D0196386

In the Dressing Room

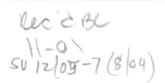

Also by Brenda Kinsel

40 over 40: 40 Things Every Woman over 40
Needs to Know about Getting Dressed

In the Dressing Room with Brenda

A Fun and Practical Guide to Buying Smart and Looking Great

by Brenda Kinsel

WILDCAT CANYON PRESS
A Division of Circulus Publishing Group, Inc.
Berkeley, California

In the Dressing Room with Brenda: A Fun and Practical Guide to Buying Smart and Looking Great

Publisher: Tamara Traeder
Editorial Director: Roy M. Carlisle
Marketing Director: Carol Brown
Managing Editor: Leyza Yardley
Production Coordinator: Larissa Berry
Copyeditor: Jean Blomquist
Proofreader: Leia Carlton
Interior/Cover design: Jenny M. Phillips of JuMP Studio
Typesetting: Margaret Copeland/Terragraphics
Typographic Specifications: Body text set in Cochin 11/15. Heads set in Mrs. Eaves Italic.

Printed in Canada

Library of Congress Cataloguing-in-Publication Data
Kinsel, Brenda, 1952-
    In the dressing room with Brenda : a fun and practical guide to
  buying smart and looking great / by Brenda Kinsel.
       p. cm.
    ISBN 1-885171-51-X (alk. paper)
       1. Clothing and dress. 2. Clothing and dress--Purchasing. 3.
    Fashion. I. Title.
  TT507 .K57 2001
  646'.34--dc21   2001017776

Distributed to the trade by Publishers Group West
10 9 8 7 6 5 4 3 2 1

Contents

Dedication

To my dad, Don Reiten, who can't match a shirt
to a tie without my mother's help. But it hardly
matters. He always looks so handsome, decked
out in the God-given jewels of love and wisdom,
humor and humility. Now *that's* style.

Acknowledgments

Thank you to my clients for the years of allowing me to look at you and your lives through my close-up fashion/style/love lens. Working with you and your wardrobes continues to be my joy, my inspiration, my teaching. Designers and salespeople who meet you always tell me, "Brenda, you have the *best* clients."

My deepest appreciation goes to my family members who accept and love even my crankiest self during worrisome deadline time, especially those nearest and dearest, my kids. To Trevor: Nights out to hear you play jazz at the Savanna Grill with the Klein Trio always opens my spirit. You're a love. To Caitlin: Caitykinola, you are the wisest seventeen-year-old I know. You being you inspires me and my friends to no end. Erin: Thanks for the pampering and entertaining weekends hanging out with you and your pals in San Diego and the sweet gifts you secretly arrange for me. You kids are the stars in my bright sky. Love you all 10,000 tons (do you mind me borrowing your line, Erin?).

To my parents, Don and Alma Reiten, who in this year of incredible personal physical challenges, always find the time and the strength to give their daughter the encouragement she needs. Your faith in me astounds me. Your love is endless. How did I get so lucky?

To my sweet bros, Kirk, Todd, and twin bro Brent—love you! To Wendalyn, my favorite sis-in-law, where's the underwear you promised? Special shout outs to Jessie, Carly, and Anna— you're always in my thoughts.

To a lovely person who on a weekly basis, got a real earful— my writing buddy, Christie Nelson. You poor dear. All those crappy beginnings that you endured with great strength adding your cheery outlook, constant good feedback, and at the home-stretch, your mantra to me, "Buck up buckaroo," was the glue that held this project together (and all others, by the way). If I start today, maybe I can adequately thank you by the year 2031 when we will be together still, shopping for scarves at the Nordstrom accessory counter, while still meeting at the Book Beat on Wednesdays at 4:30 to critique each other's writing.

To special friends, Linda Anderson and Randi Merzon, who single-handedly ripped my appointment book from my hands each month and fiercely created spaces in my schedule to write. I can't imagine how crazed I'd have been without your tough love and your gentle love all along the way. You girls rock! Leather is definitely YOUR color. What a magnificent manifesting team!

A special thanks to the best crew at the Fairfax Coffee Roastery who's there at 6:30 A.M. with smiles, good cheer, and yes, my double shots of espresso to start my writing day. Love and thanks to Kym (you stylin' cool chick you) and to Coffee Shop Guy. Your pep talks and funny quips are nothing compared to your deep friendship.

Dear lovely friends who celebrate the high times and supply Kleenex during the low times—Louise Elerding (immeasurably), Pattiricia Clure, Linda Scheibel, Kim Connor Kuhn, Toni Bernbaum, Helena Chenn, Cat Prince, Carl and Marie Dern, Cheryl Little, Cheri Hoggan, Ellen Rankin, Robert Moore. I love you guys! To Persia Matine who besides being an outrageous friend, also does the most magnificent job "makeuping" my clients. You're the best!

To my 7 @ 7 group—Christa Ortman, Joan Owen, Nadine Narita, Joanne Harwood, Kate Ames Comings, and Rosemary

Shorrock—your teaching stories of love, faith and perseverance constantly light my way.

And at deadline, who should call but the Oprah Winfrey Show. Scrap writing and fly into overdrive. A dedicated crew of ever faithfuls said yes to being dos and don'ts for Oprah's audience of 7 million. Thanks to Sheila-Merle Johnson, Diana Smart, Carol Brown, Christie Nelson, Helena Chenn, Persia Matine, Kim Connor Kuhn, Teresa Wootton (double thanks for double don'ts), Catherine Commins, Camille Chamberlain, Pam Howard, and Caitlin Kinsel.

And on to my partners at Wildcat Canyon Press. Ah yes, my editor Roy M. Carlisle, a gem to work with. Thank you for always being available and for being an understanding friend, not just a terrific editor. My precious Leia Carlton—I miss you, Sweetheart! To the bold and the beautiful Carol Brown—you're the bomb, Girlfriend. To Patricia, Nenelle, Sherry, Patsy, Larissa, and Leyza—you do your jobs so well, go the extra mile, and always make me happy to be with you Wildcats. To Tamara Traeder, what a cutie. Let me do that again: To Tamara Traeder, publisher, and brilliant leader—your tireless dedication is award-winning. To Jean M. Blomquist—so happy to be working on another book with you.

Jenny Phillips, illustrator and designer, you are one of my favorite persons-in-the whole-wide-world list—for who you are, for what you do, and for how you do it. You are my hero. Thank you once again for being brilliant—something you do so naturally.

Thank you to my AICI buds—gosh, life without you would be dull, dull, dull. A special benefit from being a member of the Association of Image Consultants International (AICI) is to have been touched by so many brilliant educators. Thank you for all you have taught me. You are the dedicated followers of fashion and image who tirelessly research, dissect, interpret and educate.

I know this is running long and you want to get on with the book, but I have to acknowledge a crucial behind-the-scenes contributor to this process. It's music. Me and my orange iMac rock in the studio, words hitting the screen with great beats in the background. The top seven CDs that have been by my side throughout the writing of this book have been Lucinda Williams, *Car Wheels on a Gravel Road*, Shelby Lynn, *This is Shelby Lynn* (thanks Hugo), Bill Frisell, *Good Dog, Happy Man* (thanks Paul), Lee Williams and the Spiritual QC's, *Love Will Go All the Way*, Keb' Mo', *The Door*, and the soundtracks from the movies *Wonder Boys* and *Random Hearts* (Dad, was that a tear in your eye? Oh, you were just yawning! Well, Mom and I liked it).

Finally, as Carolyn Huggins sings so beautifully in one of her solos in the beloved choir at my church, Glide Memorial United Methodist Church in San Francisco, "Thank you, Lord, for all you've given me." Thank you, Lord.

A Word from Mary Michael

In college my boyfriend's roommate called me the "Sweats Queen." Clothes were all about functionality—they aided me in sports, provided comfort in their soft, flannely way, and protection from the rain and cold. On the weekends short skirts and red shoes came out to attract the boys.

When I met Brenda my range of materials was pretty much: cotton. My range of colors: white, black. In our first meeting Brenda asked me to bring pictures out of magazines of things that I was attracted to. I chose many of my old standards—cool jeans and plain, plain sweaters, but then amazingly I veered into dresses with beads and shears sleeves where a bare arm showed through—fabrics that billowed. I said shyly, "I'm drawn to these things, but I would never wear them."

Brenda has kept encouraging me to uncover what it is I love. Long after those college weekends, I think I was mostly trying to hide or blend in my clothes; therefore, I had pushed down what I was truly drawn to. I had no idea. It's an amazing feeling to begin to know what it is you love—it begins to give you a particular, vivid human shape all your own.

My first season shopping with Brenda—I tentatively forayed out into color. Browns and grays. You'd think I was walking around with one of those rainbow flags draped over me with how exotic I felt. I found out that browns and grays bring out my eyes, and that I like to have my eyes brought out. Lace began showing up in the periphery of my outfits—cuffs, neckline, back. Brenda spotted me tentatively running my hand down a long, brown silk dress. She took it off the rack. Subtext: You can actually wear this! This was different than in college when I wore red shoes (I hate red shoes!), this time I wasn't so much trying to attract a certain kind of attention, I was beginning to express something really primal and womanly. This was scary for a staunch tomboy.

Working with Brenda I feel something burgeoning inside me. Sometimes trying on something that truly expresses well, me—a soft look comes over Brenda's face. I don't think I'm exaggerating in calling it rapture. That's how deeply she sees the hidden power of clothes, that somehow they can express a person's essence. With her looking at me that way, I am undoing years in dressing rooms—as a teenager fighting my mother to not wear "preppy" clothes but then making disastrous, tacky choices I saw reflected in her disapproving eyes, or years when dressing rooms meant looking for flaws. Here was someone giving me new messages: You look great. Trust yourself. Vernacular: Go girl!

Working with Brenda, I have developed a practical eye—I notice now when seams don't lay flat or if something doesn't hang right. Things that used to mystify me. I've learned a new language: I say tensil, silk, cashmere, rayon. I have learned that I love hoods and clunky, boy-shoes even when I'm wearing something feminine, as if I still want to keep my ground. I actually have fewer clothes now that I'm working with Brenda, but I actually wear them all.

Sometimes I stand looking at my closet, the sweep of color amazes me—blues but mostly now a range of rust and orange and peach and maroon. There is an underlying question to clothes now: What do I want to express? Who am I? In truth, something essential to my clothes wearing hasn't changed. I'm still drawn to simplicity. I have a low tolerance for anything too "hip." I didn't buy a beaded, sheer dress either, (maybe because I have a shedding dog that likes to drag me through the mud at the park). But who knows, it might be in my future. The poet Mary Oliver, says "You have to only let the soft animal of your body love what loves." I feel like Brenda in her way has told me that a thousand times. I'm sitting here writing this in the softest, rust colored sweater. One with a hood.

Introduction

THIS BOOK WOULD HAVE no life at all
if not for the body of clients that
have trusted their fashion life to me for over fifteen years. These
clients represent women from their teens to those in their nineties
(which proves my point that we never stop being interested in
clothes and how they make us feel), who range from a size 0
petite to a woman's size 3X, with budgets for shopping ranging
from $500 to the unlimited sort.

There are few things that are more intimate than bringing a
stranger into your closet and your underwear drawer. For this
risk that every client has taken with me, I thank you. Although
everyone thinks that their secrets and idiosyncrasies are theirs
alone, it's not true. Nothing surprises me. As different as we are,
as different as the opportunities we have to wear clothes, we are
so much alike.

We all wear clothes. We all have adventures in our clothes.
We all take our clothes off at the end of the day. In the morning,

we start the process all over again. Getting dressed is an ordinary thing and it is an extraordinary thing. Women tell me stories of what happened when they wore that red dress, what they were wearing when they met their sweetie, their favorite outfit from the 80s, the boots they wore during their whole third pregnancy, the necklace that broke and broke their heart at the same time.

Clothes mark the **journey** of our lives.

They are attached forever to important events and they make the unimportant events memorable.

As life takes its snakelike trip through time, going here and then going there, I am for many people, in the background, preparing them for what's visible at the next turn—their high school reunion, their job interview, their third job interview in a year, their new work environment, their day in court, their wedding, their trip to Turkey, their trip home to meet his parents, their date to the opera, the movies, skiing, the business picnic, the funeral of their father-in-law, their honeymoon, their holiday parties.

It is the cumulative knowledge of bodies, of how fashion works, of solutions to wardrobe crises that has come from all those clients that I bring to you. These women, my dear reader, bring you their experience in order to make your life in clothes more pleasurable and functional than it is right now. Thank them.

If we are here to teach what we need to know, I have some ideas about why fashion chose me. I remember the look and feel of the dresses my mother made me when I was young. I remember how pretty the women were in Ladies Aid meetings that my mother brought me to at our church in Hastings, North Dakota which had and has still a population of seventy-five people.

I remember when a woman came to Hastings visiting from Norway and how beautiful and different her clothes were. I sat at her heels all night, marveling at her style.

When I was a junior in high school, the mother of one of my friends coerced me into applying for a position on the local teen board at the biggest department store in Fargo. Before the application had reached the office, I was called by that friend's mother and told I had the job. She was head of personnel. That year when I was working on the fashion floor at the store (and not on the runway), helping other teens put their back-to-school outfits together, I was in heaven. I remember sitting on the floor of the dressing room with them, dressmaker pins in my mouth, marking the hem of the skirt to just the right length. Helping others get their clothes right and making it possible for them to completely forget about their clothes made me happier than anything.

A few life turns later, I was living in California. I searched for a way to express art. Every night before I fell asleep, images flashed under my closed lids like a slide show of runway fashions. I wanted to capture those images. I began to create wearable art, wearable clothes that were in themselves pieces of art, that was shown in art-to-wear fashion shows and in art galleries.

After about fifteen years, I found myself back on the floor of dressing rooms with pins in my mouth, finding just the right hem length for clients, creating "art" on the canvas of ordinary, extraordinary women. I was fascinated by how clothes could express personality.

Then came a divorce, a life-changing experience. Divorce forces reinvention, a look at new identities, and creates opportunity for fresh starts. It's a time when you have to look hard and dig deep to find your strengths, your talents.

Many clients have faced similar rough times through the death of a loved one, threats to one's health, moves, loss of jobs, marriage, dreams. Things they took for granted have disappeared. The figure that wasn't good enough when they were twenty-five is the one they'd die for at forty-five, fifty-five, sixty-five. Trademark great hair has fallen out during chemotherapy. Waistlines disappear, bodies have changed in reaction to drug side effects, a change in schedule making exercise difficult, the beginning of menopause, or maybe changes due to the nature of getting older. Elective surgery doesn't always give the anticipated results. Things come and go. **Life is fluid.** Reinvention, rediscovery, and renewal are tools to bring out often. How we get dressed can identify our response to change faster than even therapy sometimes. Looking and deciding how you dress your outsides can profoundly affect how you feel on your insides. Getting dressed is powerful medicine.

While you are dressing your body consciously, become a fierce advocate for your precious self. Develop the practice now of loving yourself as you are. What you are attached to won't last. Your love for yourself "as is" must be unconditional, not based on a number on a bathroom scale, a measurement of a thigh, or any line in your face that you see in the mirror and don't like. That is unkindness. Don't hold your love back until you lose five pounds, get in shape, have your eyes done. *Practice* love for yourself as is now, freely, generously, outrageously. Practice love.

Women have practiced self-abuse and self-hatred for years. That critical nagging mean voice has touched every woman I know, has made her feel bad about herself. It is an epidemic. Your daughters, your nieces, your cousins, your friends, maybe even you have suffered from bad body image and it is manifested in ways that are life-threatening. This frightens me. How do we retrain ourselves to speak highly of ourselves? How do we practice loving acts to ourselves? How do we teach young girls to love their bodies just as they are?

In the early weeks after the divorce, I noticed that the kids seemed to have gotten into a habit of bickering with each other. I'd hear it in the car, dropping them off at school or picking them up. It would be present while shopping together for groceries, getting ready for school in the mornings, just about any old time.

I couldn't stand it. I started calling weekly family meetings, more often if necessary, to handle conflicts. Before we got to the agenda of the meeting, we did "appreciations." Each person had to express one thing they appreciated in the other. "I appreciate how you helped me with my homework last night." "I appreciate how you treated my friends when they came over." That sort of thing. Sometimes doing "appreciations" took up the whole meeting time because it took forever for each of us to come up with four "appreciations." Those were tough times!

But you know what? It changed. With practice. Appreciating each other got easier and easier. "Appreciations" popped up outside of the context of meetings. It became easy to appreciate each other throughout the day, throughout the week. Appreciating became a habit. Problems seemed to dissolve when each family member was appreciated.

I know that "appreciations" work. It's so simple. And so hard for habitually self-critical females to do for themselves. But I ask you to help me change the world. Can you imagine the power of a whole gender that stopped criticizing itself and instead practiced self-love and lovely acceptance? I think it's possible and it may be as simple as practicing "appreciations."

Start today. Appreciate specific things about yourself. Say them out loud. Write them down on paper. Appreciate how your hair has that distinctive curl, how your eyes open every morning and allow you to see life, how your legs take you to the bus stop every day, how your fingers soothe a sore muscle. When you practice appreciation, it will get easier. And while you're getting good at this, practice adoring yourself lovingly with colors you're nuts about, fabrics that feel good against your skin, clothes that don't constrict your movement in any way.

Let clothes remind you of the **growing love** and **appreciation** you have for *yourself.*

Practice. Let that place in your heart grow wider, deeper, warmer. Practice kindness.

The best part of my job is awakening women to their beauty and to the loveliness of honoring themselves. They become better people for it. So will you. Let's change the world.

In the Beginning, There Were Fig Leaves

It's a lot like a Zen koan:
In order to forget about clothes,
you have to think about them.

"HONEY, HAVE YOU SEEN MY FIG LEAF?" Adam called to Eve from across the grove of Japanese maple trees in the Garden of Eden.

"No, Sweetie, but have you checked the forest floor? I don't know how many times I've tripped over it on the way to the waterfall."

In the beginning, it was paradise. Clothes didn't matter. Eve wasn't rushing off to the office; Adam wasn't trading stocks online. There were no bills to pay, no in-laws to impress, no performance reports to worry about. There was no shame in nakedness. Heck, there was no alternative! Not until Eve took a bite out of that darn fruit did either of them give any thought to suits, ties, shirts, belts, bras, panties, boxers, slips, nylons, socks, blouses, T-shirts, skirts, dresses, or shoes.

You might look at the first couple—before the whole fruit-snake scandal thing happened—and say those were the good ole days. But you know when someone says that, they're missing the obvious. *These* are the good ole days right now, fully clothed.

Once original sin happened and Adam and Eve were embarrassed by their nakedness, the wonderful door opened to dress-up clothes, dress-down clothes, date clothes, work clothes, gardening clothes, travel clothes, trendy clothes, classic clothes, clean clothes, and dirty clothes. We are experiencing heaven right here on earth, with clothes on.

Eve was a smart and sassy gal. I'm sure she had the vision. I think she was secretly stringing leaves together and making peplum jackets with matching skirts and accessorizing them with twig brooches that had little berries hanging from them, because it is our nature to adorn. God made us that way. Even though there may not be an exact passage about that in the Bible, I feel really confident about that fact. Eve would have had Adam in a tux by that first New Year's Eve, you just know it. It's woman's nature to decorate, to futz with things, to create something out of not much of anything. Isn't that how a lot of "Eves" hook up with their "Adams"? The light bulb goes off once she's dated him for a few weeks and she thinks, "Gosh, I could make something out of this guy!" So she marries him and gleefully dives into the project of molding a terrific guy out of an ordinary one. But wait—I'm supposed to be talking about fashion, aren't I?

For those of you who are convinced nakedness was best, let me show you how wearing clothes can feel just like being naked: you know what it's like when you put something on that's just right for your body, your coloring, your lifestyle, your comfort zone, and you go out in the world and completely forget about how you're dressed. It's out of the way. There's nothing about your clothes that distracts you or others. They just are, so you can just be. In the very same way that Adam and Eve weren't worrying about clothes, neither are you.

It's a lot like a Zen koan: *In order to forget about clothes, you have to think about them.* And if you think about them, put some time into them, then you can promptly forget about them.

Two Times
Will Do You

Have you heard the term C & E Christians? They are Christians who make a point of getting to church at least twice a year—at Christmas and Easter. That may not be your schedule, but that's about the number of times you'd need to study your wardrobe in a year to be like Adam and Eve, not thinking about clothes.

Here's what you'd have to do. Around August, you'd think about your life in clothes over the next six months and make some notes. You'd think about what you need them for, what kinds of clothes for what parts of your life, the impression you want to make in your clothes, for just six months. You'd look into your closet and see what's there that is already working. You'd say, "This is good, I think I'll rest now." After a little rest, you'd look at what is missing from your closet that, if those items were there, would make the next six months in clothes be the best ever. You would make a list of the missing items, after which, you would say, "This is good, I think I'll rest now." You'd rest for a little bit and then you'd go out and shop for the items on that list. Afterward you'd come home and say, "This is good, I think I'll rest now." After a little rest, you'd play "mix and match" in your closet to put outfits together, and you would say, "Ah, this is good. I am so pleased with myself, I think I'll rest now." And then you'd take a longer rest, drifting off to sleep with a smile on your face. You'd sleep soundly, content with these great outfits that you will wear over the next six months. And because you won't have to think about clothes, you can focus your energy on doing good deeds, forgiving others as you would have them forgive you, and fulfilling your missionary commitments or whatever else it is you do.

Time to Shop Again

Six months go by and around February, you look at your wardrobe again. You assess your needs over the next six months, over spring and summer. Maybe you are going on a cruise or a trip to Italy. You want to focus on travel clothes as well as your work and play clothes for the summer. You want a nice outfit to wear for Easter or maybe for Passover. That's fine, just put those considerations in your notes. Think it through, plan it, then go out and shop for those things on your list, bring them home, hang them up in your closet and enjoy your clothes for the next six months without thinking about them! Sounds heavenly, doesn't it?

A Little Bit of Mindfulness

What about maintenance, you say? Well, many religions include a daily practice, such as prayer, meditation, or chanting. You can take a little bit of that same mindfulness and aim it at your clothes. You notice a button about to fall off on your jacket and you calmly sew it back on. You kindly take your suit to the cleaners when it is dirty. You iron your skirt when it needs ironing, things like that. Not major things, minor things. As you care for them, they care for you.

The Price You Pay

What's the alternative? Wavering from the path of good clothing habits could be a living hell. It often is. I hear it all the time. Sure, you can ignore your clothes and shout to the rooftops, "I don't care!" Maybe nothing bad will happen right away. Maybe ten years go by. Then you wake up and your clothes don't fit you anymore. You pretend it isn't true. You try to ignore the pinching waistband and the fact that everyone around you is wearing styles you haven't picked up on yet. Your pleated skirts don't pleat anymore, but then no one's wearing pleated skirts anyway. You're down to one or two things that work for you. You block it out, hoping maybe the problem will just go away. Only when it gets painful enough—you have to go to a dinner for work and your boss is counting on you to network with prospective clients—do you face the problem: "I've gained ten pounds, I have nothing to wear." Then your devilish mind goes nuts: "I'm a failure, I look terrible, I'm never going to get this right, maybe I can call in sick, but then my boss will get mad and I'll get fired. I'm a fraud, a loser, stupid. Why am I in such a mess?" you lament.

You think about going shopping. You haven't been inside a store in years. You break out in hives the minute you get near a clothing store (at least you tell yourself you do), and so you go pull on your faithful, ratty old sweatpants and go play racquetball instead.

Only when you put it off until you have barely one-half hour to shop for something, do you dash into a store that's playing loud music. You take the advice of the first salesperson you meet, even though you suspect she's lying. You vow this will never happen again. You go to your boss's event in something that almost works, but not quite. The immediate crisis is over; you get through the dinner with the prospective clients but with no confidence because you were worrying about your clothes the whole time. Realizing the error of your ways, do you go out and buy a wardrobe that will serve you? No, you wait until you're in a more serious bind and then race again for the temporary fix that never works.

There could be other problems. I've heard them all. Your life changes. You get divorced. You move to a different state with a different climate where wool doesn't work. You change jobs and your suits don't fit in with the laid-back atmosphere of your high-tech job. Or you wake up one morning, look in the mirror and ask yourself, "Who is that person? I don't recognize her anymore."

Or, you wear your clothes to shreds. The knees are worn through your favorite pants, or the slacks you wore every day for three months are shiny as a lake in moonlight from being at the cleaners over and over. You've neglected your relationship with your wardrobe. Like any relationship, if neglected time and again, you wake up one day needing it and it's not there.

An *Answer* to *Prayer*

Is there hope? Plenty! If you just change your ways (I'll provide all the steps), the blessings that await you are immeasurable! Besides the gratification that comes from the simple practice of taking care of your wardrobe so it can take care of you, there is pure pleasure in dressing your personality, defining yourself through clothes, experiencing the scrumptious beauty of color, texture, design. There's a fashion playground out there and like life itself, the more we engage in it, the more we get out of it.

Oh yes, life has become more complicated since the original sin, but I think it's all working out for the better. Fig leaves don't come in every color, and some people really need every color in the rainbow in their closets. Also, those fig leaves would get pretty scratchy once they started drying out. And then they'd start crumbling. You'd be at a dinner party and your leaves would start crumbling, garnishing the first course. It'd be a big mess.

Now you have so many things—all much better than fig leaves—to choose from for that dinner party. And just so you won't get overwhelmed with all the choices, I'll stay right here by your side. I'll be that little voice in your ear as you go shopping. I'll guide you to make the right choice for you. I'll be there in your closet in the morning as you're getting dressed. I'll help you plan for next year, for the next job, the next marriage, the next party, the next moment. I'll work out the wrinkles in your clothes life.

I'm devoting this book to making clothes so easy for you that you can forget all about them. You'll be so comfortable in your clothes that you'll have to pinch yourself to tell whether or not you're naked.

Bren's Rules Rock

You need these rules because they come from the right source: love, common sense, kindness—something every woman needs to bathe herself in everyday

I KNOW, I KNOW—you're thinking the last thing a woman needs is another set of rules to abide by. I would usually agree with that, but not this time. These are the New Rules—the rules you wish your mother would have known so she could have shared them with you, the rules you want your daughters, nieces, and young friends to have in their hip pocket. You need these rules because they come from the right source: love, common sense, kindness—something every woman needs to bathe herself in everyday.

These new rules for dressing honor a woman from the inside out. They aren't the rules she's used to—the ones that imply something's wrong and needs fixing, rules that are telling her directly and indirectly to dislike her body. "Be nice," "Don't rock the boat," "Put everyone else first," "Don't be selfish"—these are the Old Rules for women, and it's time to leave them behind!

Plaster these new rules in every room of your home. Slip them inside every pocket and purse until you've woven them into your heart and you're living by them naturally. They are the rules I give to my clients while I'm working with them in their closets or while trying clothes on them in dressing rooms. It's my goal to make life in clothes the best it can be for them. It's what I want for you too.

Now, on to the rules. These rules rock! They're the best! Even those of you who live to rebel against rules will be attracted to these. It's a new way of thinking. I guarantee an unheralded joy and sense of peace with yourself as you begin to practice them in your life. Let's start!

Bren's Rules
for Dressing

1. **Love what you wear, wear what you love.**

   If you're not loving it, you're not wearing it. Wearing a sweater that is delicious to you cheers you up by just being inside of it. It celebrates life—your life. Wearing a sweater that you're neutral about or that bugs you—because it itches, because it was given to you by the boyfriend who dumped you for your so-called friend, because it's got a hole in it that you never get around to mending, because the color faded is nothing but a downer. When it comes to clothes, love it or leave it out of your wardrobe rotation.

2. **Dress your body graciously with no regard whatsoever to sizes.**

   Divorce yourself from numbers on hang tags. Dress for the body you are currently in. Yours, as is. Forget about what size that is. Shop for and wear clothes that fit you right now. Your essence is not a "6," a "12," or an "18." You are a fabulous person. What matters is that you look fabulous in your clothes.

3. **If clothes in your closet have expired physically or emotionally, get rid of them.**

   Your closet needs to be a gallery of favorites. If that sweater from your old boyfriend bugs you, get it out of there. If you have clothes in your closet from high school that don't make sense in your current life, get them out of there. If you have clothes with price tags still on them from three years ago and you still aren't wearing them (there's a good reason you aren't, even if you don't know what it is), cut your losses and get them out of there. All those mental distractions cut down on your love and enthusiasm for getting dressed, for living life. Clothes expire. They just do. They get outdated, they fall apart and lose their luster—or our life takes a turn and our old wardrobe doesn't make sense anymore. That's okay. **Don't feel guilty.** Make no more excuses for expired clothes and get them out of your closet. Leave your favorites. You will have fewer clothes, but remember, you weren't wearing those expired clothes anyway, so let them go in peace.

4. **Your closet is your personal shrine to getting dressed. Get everything other than clothes and accessories out of there.**

   Create breathing room. Create a friendly atmosphere in your closet so things that want to mate can, producing great combos that you wouldn't have thought of because the pool sticks and fishing equipment were in the way. Find a home for all nonwardrobe items outside of your shrine. You don't need to be thinking about half-done projects (a quilt you're making for your niece) that you've stored in there. Keep your closet neat and tidy. It makes that sometimes hectic morning time calmer when you open your closet doors and see your wardrobe neatly and clearly.

5. Put it where you can see it.

If you can't see that jewelry, those scarves, those T-shirts, you won't grab them. They want to be at the party too. Try to keep as many of your items in plain view as possible. Seeing all your options helps you create new and exciting combinations. Stack knits, T-shirts, or jeans on the shelf above your clothes rack. Remember, you don't have to get all fancy in your closet. A bar to hang your clothes on and a shelf above the bar to store what's foldable is often superior to elaborate dividers and double-hanging bars. I can't tell you how many thousands of dollars worth of closet "design" I've had ripped out of closets and replaced by a single bar. Most often, simpler is better. This is one of those times.

6. Don't save anything for good.

Good is right now. Rip those tags off and wear that new outfit for five days in a row. Break it in fast. Life is marching along. Do not hesitate. Be marching along with it in your "good" clothes.

7. Start each day with great underwear.

Just because. Working your way from the closest thing to your skin to the layer that's farthest away is a reminder of how special and perfect you are. *All* layers count. Even the ones that don't show. Extra blessings come to those who wear great underwear.

8. **If it's exercise-wear, wear it to exercise in, not to go grocery shopping in or any other kind of shopping in.**

   I don't care how great you think your body looks. No exceptions. Get dressed in street clothes for being on the street; gym clothes stay in the gym. I mean it! There's a place for everything and your butt in spandex should not be in my face while standing in the produce department.

9. **Always remember, you're worth full price.**

   Don't get caught in the mind trap of buying everything on sale just because it's a bargain. You're worth full price, so buy it because it is glorious, because it makes you look like a million bucks, because it makes you feel special, dreamy, delicious. If you buy it for those reasons, you will be wearing it constantly, so the cost per wear will be down to peanuts. Regardless of what you paid for it, it'll be the bargain of the century.

10. **Keep your fashion feet moving.**

    Don't get stuck in a decade. Life moves forward, the months and years fly by. Be on the journey. Don't stop somewhere, get off the fashion bus, and never get back on. Some beauties from high school often stay in the makeup or the clothes that they wore in their most popular time of life, so although they may have been at the height of fashion then, fashion has moved on. Not moving along with it makes you look freeze-framed in a particular year. It looks like you stopped caring for yourself. It's like not caring for your teeth regularly: a few years go by and "suddenly" you're in a heap of mouth trouble as well as facing big bills because of your neglect. What covers your body is more noticeable than what's going on inside your mouth. If you've dropped the ball on your wardrobe, pick it up again. (Don't worry. I'm going to show you how to get back on track.) Face your discomfort and don't let grass grow under your pumps.

11. Learn to accept a compliment.

Two words—"Thank you"—are the only words you need to know and use when someone says, "Gosh, you look so great today!" No lengthy explanations to minimize your brilliant taste are required. Control yourself. "Thank you" honors you and honors the good taste of the person who complimented you. Don't spoil the moment with elaborate details about garage sales, hand-me-downs, clearance sales, blah, blah, blah, blah, blah. **You look great. Face it.** Accept it. Thank you. That's it.

12. Rules are for breaking.

But not these rules!

Get Current

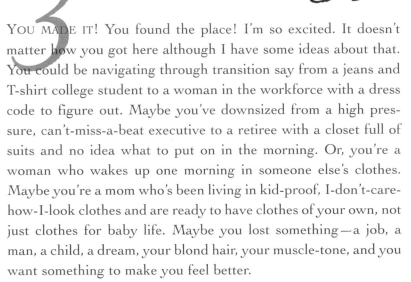

Sometimes it's easier to see what you want based on what you don't want.

3

YOU MADE IT! You found the place! I'm so excited. It doesn't matter how you got here although I have some ideas about that. You could be navigating through transition say from a jeans and T-shirt college student to a woman in the workforce with a dress code to figure out. Maybe you've downsized from a high pressure, can't-miss-a-beat executive to a retiree with a closet full of suits and no idea what to put on in the morning. Or, you're a woman who wakes up one morning in someone else's clothes. Maybe you're a mom who's been living in kid-proof, I-don't-care-how-I-look clothes and are ready to have clothes of your own, not just clothes for baby life. Maybe you lost something—a job, a man, a child, a dream, your blond hair, your muscle-tone, and you want something to make you feel better.

Things often get really bad before they get really good. (EEEGAD–I really DON'T have anything to wear!!) Your disappointment and frustration is the perfect starting point. I want to hear all about what's not working because it will point the way to what will work. Before you can dress the outside, you have to listen to what's going on inside. The adventure of getting dressed starts under the skin, not on top of it. Bring me what you've got—your healing self, your courage, your creativity and sensitivity. It's time to get up-to-the-minute current with yourself. It starts by exploring the haunting questions: who am I now and how do I want to dress myself?

If you've been out of touch with current fashion, you could feel like you've been swept up by a tornado and dropped someplace where nothing's familiar. Styles are cuckoo, fabrics unrecognizable. Aaauugh! Makes you want to give up before you start.

No-sir-ee-girl. Not to worry. This is doable. It's not as easy as getting back on a bicycle and riding. It's more like picking up a book after not reading for a long time—reading, thinking about what you read, being stimulated and inspired, and enjoying the process. It's a great read and this one's all about you—every chapter. You're the heroine. Here's the plot: You're here to love yourself. Clothes are the tools.

Get On the *Love Boat*

It's a loving act to come into present time and take your place, take your space, and be you, purposefully, now. Maybe even a new you. As we work together, we're going to address every part of your life in clothes. That's you and your clothes:

at the gym • at work • at your performances • at your dinner parties • at your board meetings • at your volunteer work at your kid's school • on date night with your sweetie • at school • in your cozy reading-at-home corner

It's everything. It's everywhere you are in clothes. And if you think, "Gosh, I'm just a mom, clothes aren't really that important,

I'm just driving kids around the county all day,"—stop! There's no such thing as "just" anything. You are a woman. You put clothes on. This is for you. You are important, valuable, indispensable. I want you happy in your clothes. This is holistic wardrobing.

A *Remedy* for the Jitters

Are you feeling nervous about just where this might take you? Well, there's one very concrete thing you can do right now to take your mind off those jitters. You can clean out your closet. It's the perfect busy work for you right now. Before you bring in the new, it's time to dump the old. It's just too hard to make sense of a wardrobe that's cluttered up with clothes that don't fit, clothes you don't like, clothes that are out-of-date and make you feel like someone in an old movie. It's time to purge, Baby, purge. Discard the bad memories or even the good memories that you've outgrown mentally or physically.

Clear everything out of the closet that isn't clothes. Your closet is going to look like a neat and tidy well-stocked pantry where you can quickly zero in on just the perfect items and put together a great dish—you! Then you can confidently and comfortably walk out the door. That's impossible if you have to weed through all kinds of things that don't work anymore.

But closet cleaning isn't always easy. I know what happens. You pull out a dress you wore to a wedding seven years ago, the wedding where you met a really cool guy that you dated. You remember where you were when you bought it, what you were thinking when you bought it. And then you're thinking about him and all the places you two went together and wasn't that Fleetwood Mac concert great and oh, the Fleur de Lys, what a fine restaurant, and two hours slip by and you're still lost in the history of that one dress.

So, here's what you have to do and be—you have to be ruthless. And here's what will keep you focused—this compelling "after" image: all clothes, great clothes, hanging in your closet, best friends begging you to "wear me, wear me today!" Every piece of clothing is ready to go, just like that—or it's out of there. Get the "baddies" away from the closet, into a box or some bags, but out of sight so you can concentrate on your goal—building a personal shrine to getting dressed. I know it's tough. I've been there, lots of people have been there, but you have to do it. Head 'em up, move 'em out.

If you come across a dress that isn't something you want to wear in public anymore but you still love it, turn it into a nightgown. Recycling works for some loved ones. If those velvet pants aren't in the "dress-up" category anymore because they're a bit worn but you love them to death and don't want to let go— okay, make them your cozy at-home pants that you wear when you curl up at night in your favorite chair with your latest novel.

Put serenity in your closet. Get everything going in the same direction— your hangers and clothes. It will make opening that closet door one of the calmest moments of your hectic life.

Dreaming Up *Your Look*

Now that you are looking at the three remaining things hanging in your closet (just kidding!), it's the right time to concentrate on what you want living in there, at-the-ready to adorn your beautiful self. There are several ways to gather that information. My experience is that your current dream dress code lives in your cells and is so close to your consciousness that you may only have to ask yourself what you want and words and images will spill out. Sometimes it takes more steps. But whether it takes just one step or a few, it's a fun and revealing process. Come on, I'll walk you through it.

I want you to have a clear picture of what *you* want. One way to get that is to write about it. The only instructions are to put your pen to paper and start writing. Don't let your fingers stop moving until you've written and written and written. Start writing, "I want" and keep filling in the blank. When you think about pausing, keep writing. Start the sentence again, "I want" and let yourself write and write and write. Then start another page with "I love" and write and write and write. Then start a page with "I need" and write and write and write. Or mix it all up, "I want . . . I need . . . I love . . ." Just keep writing.

Maybe you come up with things like this:

- I want to not worry about clothes.
- I want to have things in my closet for everything I do in my life.
- I want to express my individuality through my clothing.
- I love purple, am mad for it.
- I love shiny fabrics. I want five shiny blouses.

24

- I need something for the company picnic.
- I need to look sharper at work.
- I need to have a week's worth of different outfits to wear to work.

Got the idea? Write, write, write! Find out what's inside of you. Don't be afraid. You are gathering valuable information, needed information. How can you have what you want if you don't *know* what you want?

The "Me Glorious Me" Notebook

Okay, you are starting to accumulate some papers, and there are more to come, so I'd like you to shop for a glorious notebook — either a three-ring binder or a folder — something really special for holding all this current information you are gathering about yourself. It will be your "Me Glorious Me" notebook — something that you will refer to often, so make it sturdy.

Sometimes it's easier to see what you want based on what you don't want. If that's the case, do the Moving Away From/Moving Toward Exercise. It's always a good exercise to use to see where the heck you are and where the heck you want to be. It's easy. Make two columns. On the left write: Moving Away From, and list all the things that you're just fed up with. "I'm moving away from never having anything to wear when someone asks me out," or "I'm moving away from a messy closet where I lose stuff and I'm not able to see where anything is." Then on the right, write: Moving Toward, and in that column write all your dreams come true. "I'm moving toward having a wardrobe that works for everything I do," or "I'm moving toward having clothes that feel good every time I put them on," or "I'm moving toward expressing my joy through my clothes." Again, do not be afraid. I want to know what's in your heart. The groovy thing is that if you write it down, there really is a chance of it happening, more of a chance than you realize. We usually walk around holding all this stuff inside. Life is too short to not know your truth. This is a mind/body/heart dump. Dump it all in those columns until there's nothing left to dump.

Another writing tool that can help is the "I used to, but now I . . ." exercise. First, it's a way of recognizing what hasn't worked. Second, the "but now I . . . " part sets you up for a new behavior or a new habit. Trust what comes out in the writing. You could be very surprised. To give you an idea of how to do this, here are a couple of examples:

- I used to buy three of everything, but now I know that I never use three of everything so I'll only buy one.
- I used to wear my sweats all the time, but now I'm going to wear real clothes when I go to the market.

Another thing you can do is make a collage. Do it each fashion season and each year. Go through magazines (they don't all have to be fashion) or catalogues and cut out what you love or what has resonance. This could be color combinations, actual pictures of clothing items, words that describe what you're after — sexy, sensual, sophisticated, elegant, playful, whimsical, powerful. What is the tone of the look you're going for this year? Put words to it. They will be your guide. Again, do not be afraid!

Another great thing to do is to put words to what it is you envy in others. I know that we're not supposed to envy, but sometimes we just do. Recognize what it is you envy and write it down. I envy how my friend Sue looks put together all the time.

I envy Amy's bracelet collection. I envy the way Linda wears colors. By putting words to what you envy, you can turn around and decide to have these things in your life.

If you're thinking about doing something new and you're hesitating, do some people watching. You'll start seeing women wearing necklaces the way you've been thinking about experimenting with them and it will give you more confidence to try new things.

Do you feel a To Do list coming on? Good. Start it. Break some of these things up into smaller steps. You may want to divide parts of this project into different time frames, things you can do in fifteen minutes (some of the writing exercises), things you want a two-hour slot for (collage work), or an all afternoon piece of the project, like cleaning out your closet.

Now look at all your writings and start to distill them. Look at what you wanted, needed, and loved. Come up with a top 10, top 20, top whatever list. Drop out the need, want, love words and put your statements in present tense and embellish them until they become compelling. Don't stop until they are compelling. These will act as road signs for you on this adventure in getting dressed.

- I express my individuality through my clothing.
- I have five shiny blouses in my closet that I love.
- I look really sharp at work.

Put all of your notes, statements, and To Do lists in your "Me, Glorious Me" notebook, folder, or file. Do this now and then again every fashion season and every year to stay close to your insides. Then you can track your progress. Keep looking and revising your vision throughout the coming weeks and years. That way you'll always be current.

Now *Wait* Just One Minute

When you find yourself facing the impulse to slip back into your old ruts, read your Moving Toward exercise. It's easier to remember where you're going when it's on paper. "No, that's not the direction I'm headed. I'm headed *this* way!" Then ask yourself, "What can I do today to get headed this way?" If you said that you were moving toward having a sane closet where you could see everything, your answer might be, "Oh, I can pack my summer clothes away and make my closet more fun to open because I'd just be seeing what works for me right now."

Please remember to honor those areas of your life that are meaningful to you even if they aren't that visible to others. For Louise, the poet, it's her writing life. Until I asked her the question, "What do you wear to do your writing in?" she'd never thought about it. She spends hours each day in her office working on her writing and she wasn't honoring that time by being in clothes that really nurtured and acknowledged that part of her life. It wasn't a big project. She identified the things that felt supportive of her writing life. Pleasant colors. Cozy fabrics that are comfortable. Clothes with stretch in them as she moves to the couch, then to the computer, then to the floor.

She purchased "elegant" comfy sweats, more glamorous than ones she exercised in. She got a hooded soft sweater/jacket that zipped in front and kept her warm. She got a pair of clogs that she could easily slip into. If she has to run out and do errands when the clock strikes twelve, she's dressed casually and pleasantly and is ready to go out if need be. Like Louise, look at every nook and cranny of your life and see how clothes can support you there.

Inspired Wardrobe *Creating An* One Step At a Time

Does creating an inspired wardrobe sound time consuming? Give yourself the gift of time. It's hard to redecorate your house in an hour. You're not going to discover your personal style in clothes in an hour either. You need to manage this as a project. Commit to spending time on yourself. This is a living project and an investment of time. Set your sights on having a wardrobe that works in all areas of your life. What steps become apparent to you that when taken will help you reach your goal? Taking action—even a very small step—keeps you moving toward what you desire. You are worth the time it takes to do this.

It's easiest to approach creating an inspired wardrobe one season at a time. Keep clothes in your closet for just the season you're in. Don't tackle your whole wardrobe—unless you're totally inspired to. So if you're starting this project in the winter, do everything you plan to do—sort, dump, shop, put outfits together—for winter. Save the spring/summer clothes for when you hit that season. It'll make more sense to you. Focus your dollars on the current season too. If you spend your wad on August 15 on summer sales and put those clothes away on September 15, you're going to have a chilly fall!

One last tip: When Persia, a makeup artist and friend wants to update herself, she uses what she calls a cheating tool. She says, "The biggest cheating tool to figure out what works for me is to look at current magazines that show actresses, singers, movie stars, people really in the public eye. I look at what they're wearing, look at their shape or coloring, and I feel like they're a role model. I look to see if someone has my coloring. What do they do to show it off? If there's someone's style I really like, I copy that. It could be the way they wear color, the shoes they wear with their clothes, their shawls or toenail polish. I go into my closet or go into a store and pull that look together. I mimic someone who's paid a fortune to look glamorous and chic."

Here's what you have to look forward to once you have spent some time thinking, writing, planning, and getting current.

When you **focus** your attention
on what you **really love**, **want**,
and **need** and then you go for it,
you'll discover the **glorious satiety**
of having one **fabulous** thing
that you *lovingly wear and wear.* Doesn't that feel much better than having lots of clothes you never wear because they just aren't satisfying?

I want you satisfied.

Looking for Distraction

All those pesky details
that aren't smoothed over
before you walk out the door
are what distract people
when they encounter you.

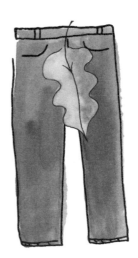

I'M SITTING IN A NAIL SALON, getting a manicure. This woman walks in wearing white pants so tight you could count her goose-bumps if it was cold enough. When she turns to go and choose her pedicure color, I can't help but stare at her butt. I'm looking for the answer to my burning question (you would have had in your head too): Is she wearing underwear underneath those skin-tight white pants?

I'm talking to a television producer and the sleeves on her jacket are hanging down to her cuticles. Does she come back to work after lunch with food all over the ends of those sleeves? They must drag across her plate. Is she doing that for effect, or does she really not notice that those sleeves are dragging my eye, and yours, to her hip line and staying there?

A blond-haired woman gets out of her car in the parking garage and starts walking ahead of me toward the elevator. Her jeans are living up her crack. Isn't that uncomfortable? Doesn't she feel that hard seam up there? Is she going to reach back and pull it out before she gets into the elevator?

I've been on both sides of these scenarios—the viewer and the wearer—well, not the white pants one. I haven't found a way to be comfortable in white pants other than by wearing something long enough to cover the whole is-she-or-isn't-she-wearing-them portion of the body. Here's why I bring these things up. All those pesky details that aren't smoothed over before you walk out the door are what distract people when they encounter you.

No Talking Behind Your Back

When I work with a client, I am looking at every detail. When she's doing it right, a woman is noticed— *"Gee, she looks great!"*—not her clothes. A woman will run into a lot of people in a day. Her audience could be the folks standing behind her in line at the coffee shop, the receptionist at the office she's calling on, the president of the company she works for, the managers that are under her in her corporation, the guy at the water cooler who's checking her out, her kids at the school play, and the parents of her kid's friends who are at the play too. I want no low-level conversations to be going on with the people she encounters as a result of some pesky detail about her appearance that could have been prevented. I want them to be seeing this beautiful woman, her intelligence and capability—and that's all.

Of course, there's always the possibility of walking out of a rest room with toilet paper attached to your heel. That's a distraction that could happen to anybody. But I want you to look at the things you can do something about. What can you catch before you walk out of your dressing room that will keep people from getting snagged on something negative about your appearance? Let's take a look and see what we can see.

Look in a full-length mirror. If you don't have a full-length mirror, put buying one on your To Do list now! Have it in your room by the end of the week. If you've noticed something, anything, count on others noticing it too. I've been in closets when a client tries to convince me that if she just wears a skirt backwards, you won't see where that bleach stain took the color out of it because it'll be in the back. However, since we see in 3-D and are not captured still as in a photograph, that's just not good enough. If it can't be repaired, get it out of the rotation of your clothes so you won't be tempted to grab it.

Looking in the mirror, how does your bustline look? Are you wearing a knit top? If you are, walk a little and watch your bustline. Are you jiggling? Are you seeing your bra's lacy pattern through the knit? Are your nipples showing? If you're in business, the last thing you want people focused on is your bustline. If you're wearing a knit top, wear a T-shirt bra, one that is smooth so the knit will grace the body. Some T-shirt bras have a softly padded cup which will keep nipples from making their presence known. If you have particularly stubborn nipples, one trick is to cover them with a Band-Aid. I'm serious. If you're wearing a jacket (that you aren't planning to take off), you're fine. But if you're giving a presentation in front of a group, please, no nipple action. People can't help themselves. They will be distracted.

Other culprits:

* **Clothes that strain at the seams** have the "Has-Mary-put-on-weight?" look.

- **Skirts that are short and when she crosses her legs you can see up to there.** "Is that white underwear she's wearing?" Really, it only works in the movies if you're Sharon Stone and your character has a reputation like hers did in that unforgettable scene in *Basic Instinct*. See how much we talk about clothes-related things? That scene, when she crosses her legs and we see she has no underwear on, will probably find a way to her tombstone. It was unforgettable!

- **Something about you that is clearly from another decade** — a shaggy haircut from the 70s, big football-shoulder padded jackets from the 80s, the big oversized layered look from the early 90s. These looks lead people to ask, "Where has she been? Doesn't she know time has marched on? Did she forget about herself?" Don't lead someone to question your credibility by looking dated.

- **Tags on scarves.** Believe me, you won't be prosecuted if you dare to remove those tags that tell you what the scarf is made of and how to care for it. Clip tags off close to the seam with a manicure scissors, or use a seam ripper and carefully pull out the threads that keep those tags attached. Then staple the care instructions to an index card with a description of the scarf and file it in a file box along with other instructions for clothes you own and need to remember how to care for. Put this box in your laundry room and refer to it before you try to wash the scarf yourself or send it to the dry cleaners.

  You may never actually clean that scarf in its lifetime, but I want you to have no excuses for **NOT** taking that darn tag off. You have a beautiful scarf and you're putting it with a beautiful outfit. Let's just focus on the beauty and not the tag, okay? There's no status in those things either, so forget about showing it off, even if it is a Hermes.

- If labels are showing through your clothes, like a black label sewn in the back or along the sides of a white sheer sweater or a white linen shirt, cut the tags out. If tags are flipping out unto your neck all the time, cut them out. Remind yourself of the care instructions in that handy file in your laundry room.

Dahling, *You Look* Fabulous

Look in the mirror. Study yourself like it matters. It does. If something grabs your eye and it's not your brilliant self, then you've got work to do. Is a hem sagging? Does your shirt have a stain on it? Is your belt cracked from using it for months (years) on a hole that you don't use anymore? Do your shoes need shining? Resoling? Replacing?

I want people to look at you and see "fabulous." I don't want anything getting in the way of that. So look at your clothes and your accessories consciously. What shape are they in? You see, not only do these things distract other people, they also distract you! They occupy space in your consciousness that could be used for something more delicious. If the top button on your raincoat was hanging by a thread and then you shored it up with a safety pin, you're going to worry about it: Will it rip off and ruin the fabric, or will someone see the safety pin? If you're not worrying, you'll be getting mad at yourself for neglecting this thing because darn it, it's still raining. Then it is easy to feel stupid or worse. It's taking way too much of your own attention. Your mind doesn't need to go to those places. Be proud! I'm proud of you! I want everyone seeing the best of you and those darn little meaningless things that end up meaning something to you or someone else need to be taken care of. You're worth it. Get rid of these distractions. Be distraction free.

You want clothes and any details about them to be out of the way so you can get to your business, so you can get on with what you're up to in life. If a distracting appearance enhances your message, then you may be in a different category than most folks. For example, wearing super tight black leather pants, a studded belt, earrings coming out of every orifice, breasts falling out of a ripped T-shirt worn inside out could be distracting for a purpose, creating the message, "I'm very different from you and I like it like that." Maybe this person gets paid the big bucks because she's the singer in the band that opens for gothic rocker, Marilyn Manson, and this distinguishes her from Britney Spears, then okay, that's fair. She'll get lots of attention and she'll sell more records. Or not. But she made her point. It's working for her.

But what about the rest of you out there? If you insist on wearing white pants, wear thong underwear in a nude color. Get yourself a pair of pants that are longer in the rise so they don't hug your butt crack. Get your sleeves shortened on your jackets that you wear at work (no reason to worry about dangling them in your salad at a business lunch). Let those sleeves be longer on a sweater for some drama when you're socializing with friends. Cut those tags off your scarf. Don't be jiggling in that bra when you walk. Wear clothes that fit you, and if you're wearing short skirts, keep your knees together.

Does Size Matter?

*What is size? It is the best
(but not perfect) gauge that
manufacturers use to assist you in
purchasing clothing that comes closest
to fitting you, someone they
have never met.*

YOU OBSESS OVER SIZE. His size? No,
your size, your size in
clothes, and I want you to
stop it right now. Let me tell
you in two thousand ways
why you must turn away from this
hypersensitivity to size. By the end of
this chapter you will become reformed
and **not care** what those tags say.
Don't let me down.

There's been this weighty ownership about size. You'll hear a woman
say, "I am a 6" with a more compelling tone than "I am a tenured pro-
fessor."

You know how significant those
sizes are? They have as much weight to

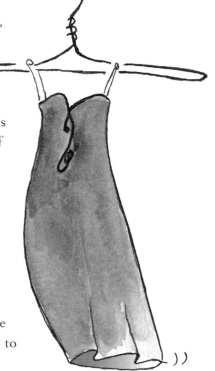

them as the number on the stub you'll bring to the shoe repair shop on Tuesday when you claim your resoled shoes.

It's not going on your gravestone. "Here lies Ellie Johnson, devoted wife, mother of four, and a size 6."

What is size? It is the best (but not perfect) gauge that manufacturers use to assist you in purchasing clothing that comes closest to fitting you, someone they have never met.

Size is a guide for your mother who doesn't get to see you that often, to find a T-shirt with a fish on it that reminds you of the fun times you've had with her at Dead Lake in Minnesota so you will wear that T-shirt over and over again (especially since it fits) and think of Dead Lake, which will make you want to go back there and visit her again soon.

We want to find the right size box when we're trying to wrap a tennis racquet for someone's birthday. We want the packaging that is closest to the shape of the tennis racquet so as to be efficient. We don't want to waste a lot of extra box or wrapping paper to wrap this gift. If we buy an adult-size tennis racquet, we'll need a bigger box than if we buy a youth-size tennis racquet. Do we care whether it's an adult-sized tennis racquet or a youth-sized tennis racquet? No. We just care about wrapping it.

If you're in a new size, should you give yourself a bad time for it? No. If you have been wearing a size 12 pant and you fit better in a size 14 pant this year, bless that size 14 pant. It is doing a much better job of fitting you than the 12 did. We are so happy about that.

Is wearing a size 14 pant instead of a size 12 pant a reason to hate oneself? Of course not! That is ludicrous! Do women freak out if they go up a size? Yes. Is this ludicrous? Yes! It's just a different fit. Do you give your friend a bad time for being one year older? Something she just "is"? No. Do you give your mother a bad time for having smile lines? Something that just "is"? No. Get off your back for just being as you are.

2000 Reasons

Here's what I want you to practice—neutrality. You're out shopping and you see the hang tags with sizes on them and they're all neutral. No favorites. They just are.

When you're shopping for clothes, what are you going for? Fit. What's the reason for sizing? To guide us to the right fit. How do you feel about those numbers that are guiding you? Neutral. No big deal.

If you were used to finding things to fit you and they were a size 8, what is your response to buying a size 6 that fits you? Neutral. It means nothing. It's meaningless. You have not found a cure for pancreatic cancer. You have not climbed Mount Kilimanjaro. You have not written the definitive book on the history of jazz. You have bought a skirt and it had a number on it, different from other numbers you're used to. Now you have a new skirt. Fabulous.

Maybe some facts will drive it home. When we were growing up in junior and senior high school, we were most likely wearing sizes in the odd numbers—1, 3, 5, 7, 9, 11, 13. Those odd-numbered sizes were Junior sizes. Generally, Junior clothes are designed for a shorter-waisted figure with a high bust (small) and small hips who is approximately 5'4" to 5'5". Can grown women go into Junior departments and shop? Yes, cautiously. I was at a party at the beach and one of the guests heard what I did. She got sheepish and admitted that as a fifty-year-old, she was still shopping in the Junior department and what did I think of that? Guess what her body looked like. She had small hips, a small bust, was just over 5'5" and had a short waist. Her body proportions matched the body proportions of a fourteen-year-old. Of course she could shop in the junior department, cautiously. She needed to avoid any obvious "childish" looks and go for things more appropriate for her age, but that was doable.

I said, "Go for it!"

For most adult women out of their teenage years, their bodies have matured. You have found yourself in another department where the clothes fit you better. Those sizes read even numbers 0, 2, 4, 6, 8, 10, 12, 14, 16. They are called Misses sizes. They are designed for the woman that is 5'5"–5'6" and has a fully developed figure (that means she has curves and fullness in places) and is of average height.

Remember that all design houses use their own standards for their "average," so Dana Buchman's average can be expected to be quite different from Calvin Klein's average and different again from Giorgio Armani's average.

Then maybe the Misses sizes stopped working for us and we felt better in sizes like these: 14W, 16W, 18W, 20W, 22W, 24W, 26W. The W stands for Woman. The difference between a 14 and a 14W is that the 14W will be cut approximately two inches wider than the standard 14.

There are petite sizes in Misses sizing and in Women's sizing, which are identified by a "P." These are cut smaller in proportion to fit someone under 5'4".

When a designer is designing a line, he is basing that line on a fit model, an actual person that he is fitting his patterns to. He experiments with his ideas for his line on her body. She is the sample that all sizes will come from. Maybe that fit model has a long torso, long arms, and long legs. Once the samples are made that fit this fit model, then the designer grades the pattern pieces up to accommodate the variety of sizes in the line. So all the sizes, whether it's a 2, or a 10, or a 14W will have started from that fit model with the long legs, long torso, and long arms. When you go to try those clothes on and you are short-waisted, average height, and average arms, you'll have troubles with the fit. Some of that is fixable, some of it may not be. If it's not working, don't take it personally. Move onto a different designer and keep trying things on until you find a fit that is closest to your body shape. Remember, they've never met you before, and the manufacturer is just doing his or her best to find something that you will like and wear.

Am I up to 2000 reasons yet why you must ignore sizes? Let me keep going.

Reason #1995: There's the client that I went shopping for one afternoon. Before the day was over, she had a fall wardrobe that fit her terrifically. That wardrobe was made up of sizes 4, 6, 8, 10, and 12. It ranged five sizes. Is she a "4," a "6," an "8," a "10," a "12"? No, she's a woman who has a great wardrobe. Size doesn't matter.

Reason #1996: I love when I'm working with a client and I get to shop with her at stores that carry sizes 14W and up. Why? Because the clothes are terrific! Manufacturers are responding to the fact that 62 million women are size 12 and up. You might not think that by looking at fashion magazines where the models are grossly different specimens, thinner than a flagpole, less meat on them than beef on spare ribs. Come on! They are usually teenagers and they have teenage bodies. Designer marketing teams are using those bodies as hangers to display clothing. You know how thin a hanger is, don't you? These models are the closest thing to the size of those hangers. They are doing a job. They aren't suggesting you look like them, they are just showing you the clothes. You don't have to look like the displays that clothes hang on.

Reason #1997: Stop trying to fit yourself into a smaller size. Go bigger! If your anguish is that you want to think you are thinner than you believe the size indicates, then go bigger! Wearing a bigger size makes you look smaller. Movie stars know this, I know this. Having "ease" in the fit of your clothes makes you look fitter, slimmer, healthier, happier. Tighter makes you look fatter. Get out of that 12 and into the 14!

Reason #1998: Style does not come with height and weight requirements. A woman can have style and wear any size. Take a look at *Mode* magazine. Its focus is the average-sized woman and up. I thought I must be on another planet when I came across the premier issue of *Mode* magazine while standing in line in the market in the spring of 1997. On the cover was a gleefully jubilant average-sized woman wearing bright yellow. It advertised "Style Beyond Size" with clothes in sizes 12, 14, 16 . . . The fashion editorial pages were filled with real women in real clothes looking like they had life by the tail and were enjoying every second of the ride. As a woman, I wanted what they had. As an image consultant, I was thrilled to have a new tool.

Everyone's having fun on the pages of *Mode* magazine. I buy this magazine for clients. I recommend it over the phone like an image paramedic prescribing medicine. I pass it around in every lecture and workshop I give, and I recommend it to women of every size because of the positive message it gives. It exudes passion, adventure, creativity, love. It shows women for who they are — smart, courageous, real, sexy, stylish.

Reason #1999: You can cut all those numbers out of your clothes, you know. Cut them out and pretend that you have a custom-made wardrobe designed by a skilled dressmaker just for you.

Reason #2000: Stop longing and get on with your life. You've heard of trophy wives or trophy husbands? I come across trophy sizes in nearly every closet I enter. There will be an obviously ancient pair of jeans with years of dust collected in its fibers and when I ask about them, the client will say, "Oh, those are my size 6 jeans. I can't get rid of those!" And then, proudly, she will say, "I used to wear them," and then she'll fall into a momentary reverie. Maybe she's having a flashback of the Grateful Dead concert she was at when she last wore them. I don't let her stay there long. I snap my fingers and say, "Snap out of it! I'm sure you've got pictures of yourself in those jeans. You don't have to keep them in your closet as a trophy anymore. You're the trophy right now, a walking trophy of your current fabulous self. Get rid of the relics. Stop the longing for that other size. Be satisfied right now with this current container of your body, mind, and soul, and dress it in the most queenly fashion you know how. Stop whining! You can look great right now in this body by wearing clothes that fit it. Don't stay mentally hung up on something that was and isn't anymore. Like that size 6 jean. Forget about it!"

Does size matter? Probably, but not when it comes to you. You are one hundred percent neutral about size, now and forever.

Fashion Fung Shway?

It never surprises me that age–old practices ride alongside front–page social phenomenon.

YOU KNOW THAT FENG SHUI HAS SLID INTO MAINSTREAM AMERICA when it appears as the background setup for Neiman-Marcus print ads harking chi-chi clothing sales and is the setup for a snappy punchline in the HBO hit show, *Sex and the City*. All of a sudden, it's a hot subject on radio talk shows and Feng Shui consultants' names are flying around like therapist referrals.

It never surprises me that age-old practices ride alongside front-page social phenomenon. At this minute, Feng Shui meets IPOs. The young, kinetic energy of seventy-hour-week dot-com businesses is on one track, and on a parallel track, and just as compelling, is the hunger for ancient practices that speak to harmony and balance.

Okay, first of all, learn to say it right. It's Feng (rhymes with tongue) Shui (pronounced SH-WAY and rhymes with WAY). It's been around for over three thousand years, but maybe you've just heard the term. Feng Shui is the ancient Chinese art of living in harmony with your home, your office, your garden. By tweaking the order of your surroundings and maybe enhancing some areas of your home, you can affect the quality of your health, wealth, love life, family life, fame, and reputation.

This is going to relate to beauty here in a minute. Go grab a protein bar or some other brain food and then come back and hang in there with me for a brief synopsis of Feng Shui.

Feng Shui focuses on nine areas of life: fame and reputation, wealth and prosperity, love and marriage (relationships), helpful people and travel, knowledge and self-cultivation, career, health and family, creativity and children, and your center (your balance point). These nine areas of life correspond to nine specific areas of the home (or office, or garden).

If one—or more—of these areas in your life isn't going as well as you'd like, Feng Shui proponents believe that you can apply "remedies" to the correlating area of your home to improve things. Remedies include light (adding light to dark corners or using mirrors to encourage more light), living plants or animals, movement (wind chimes), color, and sound (water fountains).

The wisdom of Feng Shui (and what gives it that "Oh, this really makes sense" quality) is that if we are not living in harmonious environments, we could be sabotaging our well-being and good fortune. Although it's a complex subject and you could have a library full of books on Feng Shui, I want to take a piece of it and apply it now to your wardrobe.

East Meets West

Fashion Feng Shui is one of the most recent studies to come to the world of image consulting. Fashion Feng Shui (FFS) uses the same principles as Feng Shui, only it looks at that most intimate of surroundings—our bodies, and how we dress them. Now East meets West and you can get dressed the "anciently new" Feng Shui way, mixing practices that are thousands of years old with your up-to-the minute fashions. At the same time, you may discover a new language of dressing that will bring balance and harmony to your dot-com-paced day.

Are you a horoscope reader? I am. On those occasions when it fits perfectly, there's that place in my diaphragm (not *that* diaphragm, the diaphragm that sits in my midriff) that just sighs and says, "Yes! I feel understood!" There's an aspect of Fashion Feng Shui that gives me that same feeling, like someone looked into my soul, defined it, and then reflected back what that means in clothes.

A couple of years ago, I found myself creating a new fashion identity and I couldn't have even explained where it came from. It felt organic, compelling, and necessary. I was attracted to colors I'd never worn. Earth tones were making a mass exit from my closet, and marching in to take their place were black, teal, navy blue, turquoise. Friends and colleagues were befuddled. *I* was befuddled!

I bought a scarf that I loved. It was a deep gray-blue color, very hard to describe, with a wavy pattern in it that just resonated with me. I felt more "myself" when I wore it than anything else. Personally, I was in a phase of my life where I was more inward. I was writing a lot, observing a lot. I felt quieter, more thoughtful.

One day I took a class in Fashion Feng Shui and the big aha came. The instructor had us take a quiz to identify our dominant element, part of a theory that's talked about in Feng Shui, which she was applying to our very closest "surrounding," our wardrobe.

It was no surprise to the instructor (because we are friends too and sometimes our friends see us more clearly than we do) that I was "Water," and the things I was doing in my wardrobe were absolutely related to that element. Although I'm sure I've mostly related to the essence of that element all my life, this was the first time in awhile that I was really valuing those aspects of myself and living them — hence the identification to those things that relate to "Water" had become so compelling to me. I felt best wearing on the outside the qualities I was in touch with on the inside.

I'm going to have you take that quiz. Of course, everybody is different. People never fit perfectly into a box, although every time I read something about an Aries, it sure sounds like my Aries daughter. Take this ride with me into Fashion Feng Shui where we'll look at another form of definition through the five elements: water, wood, fire, earth, and metal. Then we'll make some connections from each element to wardrobe choices. You may suddenly understand why you've been doing what you've been doing successfully all this time or get a big aha about why those mistakes in your closet were just that — mistakes. One more note: If you do this test and find that you are using parts of all five elements, that just may mean that you are a very balanced person and have integrated parts of everything, which is also a very healthy and normal response.

Elemental Fashion

The five elements: water, wood, fire, earth, and metal appear in everything physical on earth, including us. Each of us, according to Feng Shui, has an element that is most dominant to us, even though we're made up of all five.

Take this test, created by Louise Elerding and Evana Maggiore, Feng Shui facilitators and fashion consultants who developed Fashion Feng Shui. Circle the adjectives under each element column that most describes you today or most resembles how others describe you.

WATER	WOOD	FIRE	EARTH	METAL
Deep	Outgoing	Passionate	Natural	Reserved
Creative	Goal-	Powerful	Conforming	Refined
Intuitive	oriented	Flamboyant	Predictable	Meticulous
Innovative	Driven	Impulsive	Authentic	Aristocratic
Sensitive	Athletic	Vivacious	Stable	Understated
Intellectual	Initiator	Magnetic	Nurturing	Elegant
Unconven-	Youthful	Mischievous	Warm	Discerning
tional	Competitive	Charismatic	Cuddly	Aloof
Sensual	Focused	Exciting	Reliable	Organized
Serious	Energetic	Fun	Practical	Precise
Profound	Active			

In this section, circle the types of places you like to go.

WATER	WOOD	FIRE	EARTH	METAL
Trendy	Action-filled	Theatrical	Comfortable	Prestigious
Artsy	Outdoors	Opening	Familiar	Cultured
Intellectual	Rejuvenating	Night	Established	Exclusive
Imaginative	High energy	Fashionable	Historical	Tasteful
Off-beat	Fun	Jet-setter	Informal	Formal
		Spectacular		

In this section, circle what you like to do.

WATER	WOOD	FIRE	EARTH	METAL
Meditate	Play	Star	Nurture	Distinguish
Create	Compete	Attract	Support	Organize

Where did you have a concentration of circled words? Don't be surprised if you are marking words in each column. We do have all five elements in us, remember, but where was there a dominance or strong resonance? Try to narrow it down to one, two categories at the most.

Now take a look at Maggiore and Elerding's guide to the color, pattern, texture, fabric, and silhouette of clothing associated with each element.

DESIGN	WATER	WOOD	FIRE	EARTH	METAL
ELEMENT	EXOTIC	ENERGIZING	EXCITING	ESSENTIAL	ELEGANT
COLOR	Black	Green	Red	Yellow	White
	Dark tone	Blue		Earth tone	Pastel
PATTERN	Paisley	Floral	Zig-Zag	Plaid	Dot
	Abstract	Stripe	Animal	Check	Oval
	Wavy	Columnar	Pointed	Boxed	Arched
TEXTURE	Fluid	Crisp	Smooth	Coarse	Opulent
	Sheer	Springy	Shiny	Nubby	Delicate
	Gossamer	Ribbed	Lifelike	Natural	Lustrous
FABRIC	Chiffon	Cotton	Hide or	Homespun	Shantung
	Silk-Velvet	Linen	Fur	Broadcloth	Sharkskin
	Matte-	Denim	Feathers	Flannel	Jacquard
	Jersey	Seersucker	Silk	Tweed	Brocade
	Rayon	Corduroy	Wool	Gabardine	Crepe de
	Fine Knit	Cotton-	Satin	Oxford	Chine
	Gauze	Knit	Taffeta	cloth	Dupione
	Loose	Tencel	Lycra	Muslin	
SILHOU-	Hourglass	Elongated	Inverted	Rectangle	Elongated
ETTES	Flowing	Rectangle	triangle	Square	Hourglass
	Undulating	Columnar	Defined	Boxy	Draped
	Style lines	Vertical	Angular	Horizontal	Curved
		Style lines	Style lines	Style lines	Style lines

I want to give you more element details as well as a one-liner about the favored décor of each element. Sometimes it's easier to put words to our personal style by looking at how we choose to decorate our homes. If you've spotted your décor style, look to see how you could translate those looks into your wardrobe.

The **WATER** element is

self-expression oriented
and likes to be different.

Your wardrobe is defined by *creative* or *unconventional styling.* You may have a more artistic or fluid look. If you wear jackets, they would most likely be left open or unbuttoned. This is not so much for comfort, but for freedom. You love the fluidity of big scarves or shawls.

While your favorite colors are black or other dark tones (think of deep waters), you don't like anything rigid or stiff. You enjoy asymmetrical design.

We may not know their true personalities, but we perceive **Joan Baez** and **Meryl Streep** to be Water people.

Your Water home or office décor would likely be innovative, artistic, or eclectic.

The **WOOD** element is

action oriented and
likes to allow movement.
Wood people are moving all the time.

Your "Wood" wardrobe has a *casual feel* or has *sporty styling.* The way you do columnar shapes (think of tall trees) could be with a sheath dress, or you might create a column of color by wearing head-to-toe one color or by looking for "columns" in clothing shapes like in stove-pipe pant legs. You'd enjoy scarves that depict flowers or fauna, or you'd wear barrettes in your hair that are flower designs. Wood people like that clean All-American look.

Katie Couric and **Meg Ryan** are personalities that appear to be Wood people.

Your Wood home or office décor would be *relaxed* and *informal.*

The **FIRE** element is

attraction oriented and likes to be noticed.

Your wardrobe styles are *dramatic* or *sexy.* You enjoy body-hugging silhouettes, revealing clothes that show some skin, or are low cut, or show the body—close fitting around the waist, the bust, or the bottom.

You like shiny reflective textures and angular shapes, which would show up in lapel points, V-necklines, dramatic style lines, or in your accessory choices. You love wearing hides or furs in shoes, handbags, or hair ornaments.

Cher and **Jennifer Lopez** display qualities of Fire people.

The Fire home or office décor would be *bold* and *contemporary.*

The **EARTH** element is

stable, likes to conform, likes to nurture, is down-to-earth. Earth people want to be comfortable and would definitely consider elastic in their waistbands.

Your wardrobe is in *classic* or *traditional styling.*

You like cable knit sweaters, tweeds, square or boxy shapes—not body-hugging. You like square watch faces, boxy handbags, more square shapes in eyewear. An Earth person could be your CPA or your conservative business person who buys clothes as an investment and keeps them around for a long time.

Earth people could be **Barbara Bush** and **Rosie O'Donnell.**
Earth décor is *conventional* and *cozy*.

The **METAL** element is
status-oriented,
likes to impress,
and is attached to prosperity.

Your wardrobe is *refined* or *elegant*. You love a meticulous-fitting jacket, and no one would find any loose threads hanging from it or even a speck of lint on it.

You like metallic finishes or polished or shimmering textures. You enjoy luxury fabrics, wearing "sweats" in cashmere, not cotton. You love a beautiful strand of pearls.

Metal personalities could be **Gwenyth Paltrow** and **Ashley Judd.**

Metal décor would be formal and ornate or minimalist.

Style Flavors

Are you excited to see the link between elements and clothing styles, or are you thinking, well, I know my element but why bother dressing with it in mind? I think there are different times in life when it is particularly poignant to feel close to our thumbprint, the unique package that makes us up. I think it's comforting when lots of things are going on to be reminded of who we are, to not lose ourselves in the busyness of car pools, work schedules, family responsibilities. When we're going through life challenges like divorce, a move to a new town, loss of loved ones, it can be a perfect time to keep reminders close to us about what we have that can't be taken away—our essence. What better way to do that than in clothes.

By understanding the distinctive nature of each element, it is also much easier to understand and tolerate others because you see what they are comfortable in. You can better understand how they look at life, how they tackle projects, what their core beliefs are. We don't have to be the same as each other. It takes all types to create the potpourri of human beings. We'd be lost without each other and all the different flavors that people come in.

Kermit the Frog used to sing, "It's not easy being green." I'm sure the Metal person might say, it's not always easy being so meticulous, or the Wood person might say, it's not easy being so driven, but we probably wouldn't trade our nature for anything else. We're familiar with our nature and I think that it is our life's plan to learn as much as we can about ourselves. What fun to use clothes, color, and texture to remind us of our nature, as a way of expressing ourselves more authentically, and to then recognize and appreciate the authenticity of others.

I've always believed that clothing is a tool for **expressing** your inner life. Dressing according to your primary element is one tool that can help you do that. It helps me.

What to Wear to Score

*The overwhelming evidence, Girls,
        is that you can keep that brain in your
head, flaunt your personality, and find
        the courage to say a few words to a
cute guy at a reception—and chances are
        that you'll score, with or without that
                glorified halter top.*

I'M IN THE DRESSING ROOM with a sharp, talented, great woman who is single. I've got her looking absolutely fabulous in clothes that bring her beauty . . . POW . . right in your face. If you were there with me, you'd be shrieking like me, "Sallie, you look fantas-tic!" Sallie looks at herself in the full-length mirror and she sees it too. Then something happens. Her shoulders slump, her chest caves in, the smile leaves her face and she whimpers . . . WHIMPERS! . . . , "I see what you mean, I look great, but it's not the look that attracts men."

I WANT TO PULL MY HAIR OUT! This woman is gorgeous. What's she talking about? What man wouldn't notice her and want to gobble her up? I argue, but of course, I'm not a man and I don't have any data to back myself up.

Women—smart women, accomplished women—are convinced there's a magic "look" that men will fall for, and it usually involves something that isn't in their closet or wouldn't look good on their bodies. They're just sure of it. Their life experience, intelligence, and interests don't mean a thing. They're sure that they have to leave those in a drawer at home and go out into the looking-for-a-date world wearing this . . . I don't know . . . this magic outfit that will get a man's attention. How did women get so insecure? Is it fostered by those banner grab lines blazing on the covers of women's magazines month after month that promise the latest trick to get or keep a man? Does this sound like someone you know? Probably every girlfriend you have? Or maybe even you?

In Search of the Magic List

It's got to stop! If women won't listen to me in the dressing room, I have no choice but to go out there and ask the men themselves. If there's a list of clothing items that "men find attractive," then gosh darn it, I'm going to find out what's on it. I'm going to help women everywhere get the dates they long for. I'll ask men to give me that darn list, once and for all, and I'll spread the word to every single woman I know. Whatever clothing items that are on that list, we'll shop for them.

The opportunity lands in my lap one night when I round up a couple of girlfriends and drive them to a jazz club in San Francisco to listen to a female singer I've been hearing good things about.

We get there an hour early and score the last three empty chairs in the place at a table for four. That's where we meet André. Handsome André, I might add. It's his table we join. He's there to hear this singer for the umpteenth time. When he hears this is our virgin visit, he lets us know what we're in for. "This is like being in a local club when Billie Holiday was singing on stage only before Billie Holiday *was* Billie Holiday," he says.

We have an hour to kill. André is Mr. Friendly. I decide to take advantage of him. "André," I say, "We've just met, but I'm wondering if I could ask you some personal questions . . . because you're a guy and everything." (You can use this as your own pick-up line if you'd like.)

"Go ahead," André says enthusiastically.

"You see," I start, "I dress women professionally and my single women clients who are looking for dates seem to think that there are magical items they could wear that men would find attractive. Only there's some confusion over which magical items those are. Mostly she thinks it has to be short, tight, and feminine. What do you think?"

My pen is poised on a paper placemat ready to capture "the list." André doesn't hesitate. He says, "It's personality. Tell them it's personality. Personality more than anything is what attracts men. What *really* gets us is a sense of humor. If someone can make us laugh, we're attracted to them."

Wait a minute. What about the clothes? Where are the clothes? This personality thing has grabbed my tongue. My single friend, Linda, jumps in and picks up the ball. "But André, if she's wearing something feminine or revealing, doesn't that attract him?" she asks.

He laughs for a full minute. "There are so many things that women think we're trippin' on—and it all goes right over our heads," he says. "If a woman wears something really provocative, she's going to draw attention. That'll get her the first two seconds, but if there's no personality, that's it."

Linda doesn't give up. She's a dog after a bone. "But don't they have to look sexy? What about tank tops and short skirts?"

André shows patience. He's probably a kindergarten teacher. He says, "If women approach men, nine times out of ten they will be successful because men are sluts. We can't say no. You can always see fairly mediocre-looking women with men all around them because they have personality. They aren't aggressive, they're assertive."

So this is *not* what I expected to hear, but it's what I *wanted* to hear.

"But what about all those articles in women's magazines?" Linda presses. "What about those?"

"You want to know the art of attraction?" André teases us. By now, we're all leaning so close to his face that we can count his pores.

"What's the art of attraction?" he repeats. "Your ability to engage another person. If you can **engage** a guy for two minutes, **you've got him**. The most **successful** women talk to men. That's it."

He leans back in his chair, satisfied.

"I'm just giving all our secrets away, " he admits. "It's more than physical attractiveness. *Are you willing to engage a man?* Some women think, 'If I show I'm smart, I'll intimidate him.' If he's intimidated, you didn't need him in the first place. I'd be attracted to a woman who had opposing views. The fact that she had an opinion would make her attractive. When you talk to us, we're not going to blow you off."

André is my instant hero. We are exuberant and the next Billie Holiday before she *is* Billie Holiday hasn't even stepped on stage yet. I have my answers. I can't wait to spread the word.

We thank him for revealing The Big Secret. He says modestly, "Hey, no problem, but really, if you don't believe me," he says, "just ask those guys at the next table. They'll tell you the same thing. Go ahead. *Engage* them. You'll see."

Me? Miss Shy? Engage them? I order another Cosmopolitan for courage. I sip on courage and then I turn to the next table. Two guys, same question. I start out, "Women want to know . . . " blah, blah, blah, positioning my pen, although I already know the answer. I'm just doing this for André.

We aren't on a first-name basis, but Guy #1 on the left blurts out, "Oh yes, we're completely looking at their clothes!

Women should wear tight clothes, clothes that hug their boobs, their butt, or their thighs. We look at how revealing their outfit is. We're interested in whether we can see skin underneath or now they have those sheer fabrics that cling to their bodies that look like skin, only *better*."

Guy # 2 on the right joins in, "She needs to wear something that will flatter her figure so you notice her figure." Their favorite clothing item on women? "The halter tops that are basically large bikini tops that you wear out at night. A woman will get three or four glances from me wearing that."

I'm stupefied, but I hang in there. "Will you go talk to her?" I ask Guy #1.

"No," he says. Then he thinks some more and adds, "Well, maybe. A guy figures you have to talk to twelve women before you get one to listen to your bull."

Guy #2 is married. Does he remember what she was wearing when he met his wife? I ask. "I *definitely* remember what she was wearing. She had on a tie-dye halter top, not a Grateful Dead type tie-dye, but really 'quality' tie-dye."

I ask his buddy, Guy #1, who is engaged, whether he remembers what his fiancée was wearing when they met? "Absolutely!" he says. "She was wearing sweat pants and a raincoat."

Wait. Sweat pants and a *raincoat*?

I turn to my pals and André. I have the list and halter tops are on the top. I feel sick and it's not from the cosmopolitans. Why hadn't I just been content with André's answers? That was the message I wanted to spread from village to village. "It's your personality they are interested in! Stop worrying so much about how you look," I'd shout. "Just be yourself! They like it when you just be yourself!"

The singer comes on stage. The place is mobbed by now. André is right about this woman. I feel like I'm watching next week's scheduled musical guest on *Late Night with David Letterman*. She's amazing! I listen to her hit high notes, low notes, and everything in between, but mostly I am thinking about André's whole "engaging" theory.

The way I met a major sweetie in my life—it happened just like André said, only without me realizing it. I "engaged" the cute, adorable, younger man at a wedding reception. It was effortless. I was certainly attracted to him, but of course, I wasn't thinking about dating him. He wouldn't be interested in an older woman anyway I figured, which made it totally easy to be my natural self. I asked him how he happened to know the wedding couple and we never stopped talking the whole afternoon. That conversation marked the beginning of a supreme love affair.

Anyway, André was right about the singer and I could see he'd been right about the engaging thing, at least in my case.

A couple days after the jazz club interviews, I meet Paul, the younger guy from that wedding reception, for coffee. I couldn't wait to tell him about the André theory of engagement, but decide, what the heck, I'll ask him the question first. *Then* I'll tell him what men think. I start out, "Women . . . blah, blah, blah, blah, blah. . . what do you think?"

He jumps in. "Women think men are into them for their looks. Young girls dress flamboyantly and revealingly. They're showing a lot more skin. That's what you do at that age. When women get older, they dress more conservatively, less revealingly."

Like André and Guys #1 and #2, Paul is eager to give me the facts.

"If you see someone that reveals everything," he says, "there's no mystery to it. But if you see a woman, say, dressed in a suit, you know that when those glasses come off and the hair comes down, you better watch out. It's like Clark Kent and Superman."

"Uh-huh," I say, writing furiously while keeping a reporter's neutral face.

He continues, "Men know that beneath the surface there's something just busting to let loose. It's kind of hidden behind the business suit, that beautiful sensual woman. We want to find out what's beneath the surface. Women don't have to be in our faces trying to look good or impress us."

He informs me, "Everyone's going to hit on the young girl with the hot pants and high-heeled shoes. But you have a lot of young pretty girls out there that have no personality, no development. We know that there's more mystery to crack with a sophisticated woman. With a sophisticated woman there are puzzle pieces. Not only will there be great conversation because she knows who she is, but there will be mystery and intrigue. A lot of men like that."

I think about being in the closet with a client who some weeks back tried on a long-sleeved, banker's gray, straight sheath dress that hit below the knee and came all the way up to her neck. She said to me that day, "It may be hard to believe, but this dress is my husband's favorite. It's the sexiest dress I own according to him." It *was* hard to believe, but now it made perfect sense.

The Cheat Sheet

Thanks to these four generous men, I think I have the answers. There are men who want to see all they can within their legal rights without getting arrested. There are men who don't want it spelled out for them, who want to use their imaginations and do some sleuthing themselves. There are those who just want to engage with another human being, explore minds, have some fun. Doesn't that just about cover all the bases?

The overwhelming evidence, Girls, is that you can keep that brain in your head, flaunt your personality and find the courage to say a few words to a cute guy at a reception and chances are great that you'll score, with or without that glorified halter top.

As your image consultant, I still have a couple of things to say to you before you walk out the door looking for that guy in a jazz club, a coffee bar, or at a museum opening. Let's get into that closet of yours first. I want to see some signs of fun in there, tools to spark up your dating life. I'm going to say it again: Dress yourself the way that makes *you* feel happy. If that's halter tops, okay, but it doesn't have to be. Wear what pleases you. Maybe you do show off some body parts. Maybe you choose to wear a close-fitting pant or a tightish sweater or a short skirt. Fine. I just want you to have some date clothes hanging in your closet—things you don't wear to work. It helps to draw the line.

Mood Enhancers

"I'm having fun now" could mean exchanging the wool twill pants for paisley velvet patterned ones teamed with a close-fitting turtleneck or a sleeveless sweater if it's hot where you're going. We're relaxing, we're having fun, so let your clothes match that mood. That can mean brighter, hotter colors—vivid orange, fuschia, hot pink, bright turquoise, lemon-yellow in place of the grays and navy blues you might wear to work. Bright, punchy colors are playful. Black is elegant and mysterious, if that's the mood you're going for. Soft pinks, peaches, and apricots are romantic colors—feminine and dreamy.

Shiny fabrics are festive. Shine can come in fabrics like a silk charmeuse or a taffeta, or in the way a fabric is woven so it seems to change colors as you move inside of it. A great fitting pair of pants with a colorful or patterned, shimmery sweater or blouse puts you on the playing field. Leave the power suit in the closet. Shimmer can come in metallic fabrics or sequins. Some flash is fun.

Next, change your accessories. Kick off your "sensible" work shoes and slip into something strappy to show off your painted toenails. Change your handbag. Use something smaller than that tote that carries half your office around on your shoulder. You just need something big enough to carry your ID, a lipstick or lip gloss, and some cash. This bag or clutch could be an interesting shape or color. It could be textured leather or suede, or made from a tapestry, a patchwork fabric, or an animal print. Wear bracelets. Wear bangle bracelets or woven metal bracelets that slip up and down your wrist. Put on dangly earrings—drop pearls or black-jet beads—something with movement so when you shake your head, there's something to catch someone's eye and hold it. Movement feels sexier than something that's stationary.

Give the Date a Chance

When you look in the mirror, spot the signs that you're going out to have fun, not that you're going to work. I'm not saying that work isn't fun, but leave that state of mind at the office and remind yourself that you're shifting gears by shifting the elements of your dress.

Try your best to avoid wearing things that hurt—shoes that pinch, waistbands that grab, bras that gouge. It can be done, but it's hard to smile and "be yourself" when you're hurting.

Have an idea of what the dress code is in the places you go out to so that you're not spending the whole night squirming in your chair and wanting to get out of there because you're not dressed appropriately. Plan ahead so you can forget about yourself and be fully present. When you're dressed appropriately, you'll relax and have more fun.

You want to know how to score? I'm going to say what I've always said, only now with more conviction and more documentation: Be yourself. Look like yourself. Engage a guy in easy conversation and see what happens. (I learned that part from André.) If you are wearing a buttoned-up suit with little or no skin showing, someone out there right now could be picking up your scent and looking up your phone number. Don't make that halter top thing big in your mind. Remember the aphrodisiac power of sweat pants and raincoats. I'd say that nearly cancels out the halter tops, wouldn't you? Don't feel that if you're not spilling the goods in an outfit, that you're not being noticed. Who was it that said, "It takes all kinds?" Oh yeah, my mother. She's right again.

Now get out there and **score!**

Capsules Anyone?

*I read a statistic once
that said women wear
ten percent of what's in their
closets. In my experience,
after nearly two decades
of being in women's closets,
I'd say that's high.*

PULLING A WHOLE WARDROBE TOGETHER that works
can be a daunting project. Wait, let's raise the stakes.
How about a wardrobe that works one hundred percent of the time? Sounds impossible? You're thinking, "My underwear drawer is barely functional.
How could I have an entire wardrobe that works?"

I read a statistic once that said women wear ten percent of
what's in their closets. In my experience, after nearly two decades
of being in women's closets, I'd say that's high. Darn high. Most
wear far less than ten percent of what's in their closets. With stats
as low as that, there's nowhere to go but up. Let's set some goals
for your wardrobe usage. Let's see, how about you go for, hmmm,
one hundred percent? It's possible, very possible. Make it your
goal and I'll help you get there. I'll give you some little capsules
that will get things moving. Don't worry. They're legal.

A wardrobe isn't built in a day. First of all, there's the mental work — if you have to get current first — and that could take a few weeks. Hey, to write a brilliant term paper (or to have a fab wardrobe), you have to do research first. After the research is done, you comb through your notes, outline your points, and then you write the paper, turn it in, and get an "A". The more you do the mental homework, research the insides of your heart and brain, and write down your notes about what's in there, the quicker the actual wardrobe comes together. We're not going for just any old wardrobe here, we're going for a **satisfying** wardrobe, an "A". I want to look at you in your full-length mirror and see the grin across your face that says, "My wardrobe knows how to satisfy me."

Small is Better

One way to have that primo wardrobe is to break it into capsules. Wardrobe capsules are groups made up of individual pieces that when combined together offer maximum use. Think small, concise, efficient. It's like taking one idea in the outline of your term paper and developing it as completely as you can so it's strong on its own even though it is just a small part of the whole term paper. If you have lots of capsules in your wardrobe, pretty soon you have a complete wardrobe that works one hundred percent of the time just like those well-developed outlined points flow into a terrific term paper. It's doable. I'm going to get you started. I'll offer you capsules for different parts of your life. You decide which ones work for you and then improvise.

Designers design in capsules every season. They create a collection of pieces that work together. They'll create suitings —

pants, skirts, and jackets—that go together. The designer will offer a couple of different styles of pants, skirts, and jackets so they'll capture a bigger portion of the buying market. They want to satisfy you and to fit you, even though it doesn't seem like it sometimes. Remember, use your power of choice, walk away and look at other collections until you find the one friendly to you, your body, and your checkbook.

Within that collection, the designer offers various tops and maybe sweaters that will mix and match with those bottoms. You can choose solids or prints. The less classic pieces are called novelty pieces. The designer may have "basics" in the line and then throw in a novelty jacket, which could be more trendy, fun, unexpected, and more memorable.

Let me talk about that for a minute. **"Basics" are those pieces that are the easiest to mix and match with other clothes.** They have fewer distinctive details so they can be dressed up or dressed down. They are less memorable. You could wear the same black suit two or three times a week with different tops and the suit itself, if uncluttered by details, will not be memorable.

You get more mileage out of unmemorable pieces. If you wear jackets with lots of pattern and bright colors, they will be memorable. Others will recognize your pineapple print peplum jacket if you wear it on Tuesday and Friday.

If you're a lover of memorable clothes, plan to have more clothes living in your closet. You'll need lots of variety to keep yourself entertained. It's easier on the eye to be around simpler design, subtle pattern, and neutral colors than it is to be around clothes that are big on unusual details, bold pattern, and are in bright colors. People famous for having few things hanging in their closets but always seem to have plenty of great outfits to wear are those that invest in neutral colors, solids, and simple design. Then they add accessories to create variety — which could be made up of plenty of color and pattern say in scarves or stoles, shoes or handbags. The accessories create interest, not the clothes themselves.

Most people don't buy a new wardrobe every season. We build on wardrobes. There are pieces in our wardrobe from a year or more ago that are in great shape that we love but we aren't utilizing. I want to capture those pieces in your closet and build a life around them.

Here's how a budding image consultant experienced this concept when she was in high school. My first aha experience with the simplest of capsules came to me when I was seventeen. My mother labored over her Kenmore sewing machine in the basement for weeks and came back upstairs with this knee-length coat made from a black and white plaid wool coat that she had worn in the 50s. I never felt compelled to choose it over my brown corduroy jacket until Christmas when my mother gave me a long oblong mohair scarf and matching gloves in lemon yellow. That yellow was redemption for that serious plaid coat and we were all inseparable until the snow melted. I bet I wore that combo for three years in a row, until I moved to Southern California and no snow. That coat, scarf, and gloves were a small capsule that made everything look good. *And* I loved it. See the **Outside Capsule** below for more on how to do this.

One place where people work with wardrobe capsules is when they pack for trips. If you are planning a travel wardrobe, you want the fewest number of pieces to clothe you for that limited period of time. You might start with one pant, add three tops that will go with it, a couple of sets of accessories, one pair of shoes, and live in it for a week and a half or two, changing the tops and accessories around for variety. That pant is the lowest common denominator of the capsule, the most basic starting place that outfits are built around.

Check out some of these capsules I've designed for you. Find yourself thinking about how you're going to create capsules in *your* wardrobe.

The Jean Capsule. Start with a great fitting, comfortable jean. Add a boot or loafer and a belt in the same color and texture (smooth belt, smooth shoes/textured boots, textured belt). Then add a turtleneck in a neutral color (maybe the shoe color), a colorful T-shirt (for variety), and a shirt in a solid color that can be tucked in or left out. Add a jacket—leather for versatility. It can dress any of these combinations up and go more places than a cotton twill barn jacket can. The jacket should work back with all the tops you've chosen. There's your casual jean capsule wardrobe. Dress it down and double the mileage by adding a more casual shoe and belt to your capsule. And then break out that cotton twill barn jacket if you'd like.

The Traditional Work Capsule. This assumes you're wearing a suit to work. You buy three pieces—the skirt, the pant, and the jacket. If you buy one that is pretty clean in terms of details, you'll have it for a good long time. Buy the best quality you can in a suit. Now, if you aren't a skirt person, then drop out the skirt in this capsule. Or vice versa, if you're not a pants person. If you use both, buy both. Now, with those three pieces you will buy three tops. A neutral blouse, maybe a print blouse, and a colored knit top. All three tops need to work equally well with the suit. That's a work capsule. A Frenchwoman buys two good suits, maybe, a year. And she wears them—over and over again. That's what you do with good clothes. Wear the heck out of them. Let this work capsule be a work horse for you.

Looking into the future, take that suit next year and the year after and look at changing the inside pieces. Your blouses get stained or worn from big-time use, so replace those each season. Maybe the first year you wore that suit, you wore neutral colors only. Maybe this year you are feeling like brights, or maybe prints, or maybe knits and not blouses at all. A basic suit can reincarnate over and over again. Add scarves or necklaces and it takes on even more lives.

The Casual Work Capsule. If your workplace is ruled by khakis, then start there. Get a great fitting khaki pant as the bottom piece. Add to it a cardigan set, an unstructured jacket, a T-shirt (to wear under the jacket or the cardigan), and a blouse (also to wear under the jacket or cardigan).

The Lingerie Capsule. Think of the robe as the jacket of a lingerie capsule wardrobe. Then create a lingerie wardrobe by picking pieces that work back to that robe. Let's make the robe a silk knee-length kimono style. Here are some pieces that could go under it:

- a lace teddy
- pajama-type bottom in silk with a pretty camisole or bustier for the top
- silk chemise slip (that you could turn around and use under skirts or dresses for your day wear)
- body suit
- thong (this would be the bare bones wardrobe plan)

Let's add some irresistible easy slip-into-and-out-of mules with maribou feathers across the front, in heels or a wedge, to any of these combinations. You're set for action.

The Outside Capsule. What you wear on the outside of your clothes is often what the majority of people see as you go about life. Take a look at your coat and accessorize it. Be sure your handbag and shoes work together with it so the outside picture is really pleasant. We'll see your shoes, your coat, your bag, and in winter, your hat or scarf and gloves. Keep them friendly with each other by blending colors or textures.

When you're putting together your outsides, consider your umbrella and your rainboots too. You're buying them anyway. Buy them in colors that blend with your coats. Or if you've got killer boots and you're buying a new coat this year, bring those boots with you to the dressing room and be sure they look great with the coat you're buying.

The Accessory Capsule. Do you have favorite necklaces that you never wear because you haven't got earrings to go with them? Do you have a great belt you love but when you go to put shoes with it, you never have the right color shoe or the right mood of shoe to go with it? Go right now to your accessories and pull out your favorite pieces that you aren't wearing. You have outfits in your closet that are dying to be worn, if you'd just finish putting them together with accessories.

I do this when I'm in closets with folks. We look through their jewelry cases, their scarves, their belts, their shoes, their handbags. And we look for the missing ingredients, the missing pieces that would allow them to complete outfits by filling in the accessory blank. Angela had a beautiful multistrand set of salmon-colored pearls but no earrings, so that necklace sat unused. She found an earring with a similar shade of pearl in similar scale and instantly it became a favorite that she wore a lot. Cathy had a chunky gold bracelet with faceted pieces of topaz going around it in links. We couldn't match the topaz, but found a gold earring in the same patina as the bracelet (an antique) that blended beautifully. In jewelry, you want to let the main piece be the guest of honor and all other supporting pieces need to just repeat an element from the main piece (color, texture, mood), but never overpower it.

Mary had an American Indian concho belt that she enjoyed wearing, but didn't have earrings to wear with it. We ended up taking two of the conches off the belt (they were the size of dimes) and having earrings made for her to create a harmonious set. Finish what you've got. It'll expand your wardrobe instantly. Your clothes will be so happy with this new addition and your wardrobe will look bright and cheery and renewed to you.

The Dressy Capsule. Thinking about what to wear to holiday parties may be the last thing you have time to prepare for in an already busy season. Plan ahead and look during the year for these key pieces—a dressy shoe, a small dressy handbag, an interesting earring, and a stole that look great together. You could add this capsule to your sweater and dressy pant, your simple black dress, your evening suit, or even your business suit, if it's simple enough to camouflage as an evening suit.

The Shoe/Handbag/Belt Capsule. Regardless of the tone— whether casual or dressy—find compatibility in your shoes, your belt, and your handbag. It can be such an easy "connect" to have them working together, and just as easy a "disconnect" to have it not working. This unifying capsule can be the boost to your wardrobe that lets you connect clothes that you otherwise couldn't. An olive pant and a chartreuse green blouse come together with a united shoe, belt, and handbag in a dark brown or a black.

Pay attention to what stops you from wearing something. If you go to put on a matching top and skirt and you get no further because you don't have shoes to wear with it, then get those shoes on your shopping list immediately. People aren't wearing what's in their closets if their closets are full of fragments. Work those fragments into capsules. They're good for your wardrobe.

And if there are some big holes in your wardrobe where there's just nothing there, we'll go shopping and buy a capsule that will fit that part of your life, okay?

Stand Up and
Be Measured

*In fashion, illusion
rules. It doesn't
matter what the
actual body looks like.
Most of us don't see each other naked,
so we can create good proportion even
if we don't have it naturally.*

WELCOME TO THIS ADULT EDUCATION COURSE: Human Fashion
Physiology. I have lots of things in store for you tonight, Class.
Susie, could you stop whispering there in the back row and pay
attention please? I see we have some sixteen-year-olds here tonight.
That's good. Better to get this information early on. It'll keep you
from unnecessary agony in the dressing room. Tonight we'll be
talking about proportion, illusion, and crotches. Stop tittering.

Bodies are not created equally. After today you'll get answers
to questions like, "Why doesn't a short skirt look good on me?"
Or, "I have lots of styles of jackets in my closet, but I only wear
one of them. Why is that?"

Bodies are long in places, short in places, curvy in places,
straight in places. If you understand how yours is put together,

you can be smarter and quicker about finding things that your body will wear effortlessly. Can I have a show of hands? How many of you would like shopping for clothes to be more effortless? Well, all of you! That's impressive! Okay, let's get started.

The first thing I want you to do is break into pairs. We're going to measure bodies with the cloth tape measures I have provided. Do not, I repeat, Do not take this tape measure and measure Around anything—like hips, waists, or busts. It is a federal crime to measure around anything on a woman unless you have a permit to do so—which you don't. It is punishable by electrocution, I believe, so don't try anything funny.

The first thing I want you to do is measure your partner's face. That would be from the top of her forehead to the bottom of the chin. The first chin. If she has a prominent hairdo that stands considerably taller than the top of her forehead, go ahead and measure into her hairline too and make a note of those numbers.

Now, take the cloth measuring tape and measure across your partner's shoulders, from socket to socket. Have her move her arm around a bit in the socket if you have a hard time finding it. It's that bony part of your body at the edge of your shoulder. Write down that number.

Now take her face measurement and multiply it be two. If her face measured seven and a half inches, then her shoulder measurement should equal fifteen inches approximately. Is it? Remember about the hair? Sometimes people who have a wider shoulder measurement instinctively wear their hair taller to make their face look more proportional to their shoulders.

Any questions? Yes, go ahead, Cynthia.

"My partner's face measured eight inches and her shoulders only measured thirteen inches. Is that bad?"

Cynthia, nothing is bad. When a face doubled is quite a bit longer than the shoulder measures, it just means that she will want to consider wearing a garment with a shoulder pad in it that will extend that line a bit and offer more balance to her long face. In fashion, illusion rules. It doesn't matter what the actual body looks like. Most of us don't see each other naked, so we can create good proportion even if we don't have it naturally. Sue Ellen, put your hand down. I know you love your nudist weekends in Palm Beach, but we don't need to hear about it again. I just want to make the point that you are all fine just the way you are. If there are discrepancies in these proportion exercises, we're here to make adjustments in our clothes to make our bodies happier wearing them. Any other questions? Margaret?

"Ellen's shoulders aren't so much smaller than her face doubled, but her shoulders slope down a lot. What about that?"

Good question, Margaret. Thanks for asking it. A sloping shoulder can easily be straightened out by adding a shoulder pad to even it out. It can be a smallish shoulder pad since you don't need to add it to extend the line, just to straighten the line. A straight shoulder line makes you look healthier and younger. It's sort of like eyebrows. If your eyebrow line fades out, your face drops and looks older. Put eyebrows back on the face and it frames the facial features and you look perkier and younger. Let's get back to proportions.

Measuring Up

Find your partner again. Ask her to slip her shoes off and if she's wearing a jacket, have her remove it so you can see her body better. We're going to measure the body in four places. Sally, what are you doing with that tape measure? Remember, **not around anything!** We're just going up and down here.

First, hold the top of the tape measure at the top of the face again and let it drop down the center of your partner's body. Now ask her to lift one arm up and find the spot under her arm where the top of her bra crosses. It would be where a seam would be in a blouse or a T-shirt, if she is not wearing a bra. With your finger, come across the body to the tape measure and see what that number is and write it down.

Next measure from that underarm to the break of the leg. The break of the leg is where your hip socket lives. Have your partner raise her knee and feel for where the hip socket is. Write down that number.

Next measure from the break of the leg to the middle of the knee and write that number down.

Then measure from the middle of the knee to the floor and write that number down.

Now you're looking at four numbers on a page, one on top of each other. We aren't interested in the numbers themselves that much, just the difference in those numbers. Where are the numbers large and where are they small? If they are almost the same, roughly within an inch or two of each other, you are looking at a well-proportioned body, one that doesn't have many clothing issues in the dressing room. Very few of these exist in the world, so don't count on finding it in this classroom. Usually, there is a discrepancy between the numbers. The more discrepancy, the more we will work with illusion to balance the body.

Okay, I see some questions on your faces. I'll make this easy for you. Think of these four areas of the body as rooms in a house. If you have a big room in your house, that's where you plan to place the grand piano or your handsome collection of antique carousel horses. If you have a room that doesn't have much space in it, or a lot less space, it's not where you're going to put your five exercise machines. No, you will minimize things in that room, keep it quiet, not bring tons of attention there.

It's the same way with the body. Where you have a bigger room, you will put more attention there. If the first room is the largest, the one from your head to your underarm, you can use that area to show off your collection of beautiful jewels. If you come across a photo of Elizabeth Taylor from head to foot, you can almost surely see that this room is her longest room. She's really quite petite and she is long in that first room, shorter in the other three. Lucky for her, she owns more jewels than Bill Gates owns stock in Microsoft, because her chest is the perfect canvas for them. You know how they say there are three things you have to know about real estate — location, location, location? Elizabeth Taylor knows location.

Go over this number with your partner. If she's short there with "no room in the inn," then these are several things that she could do:

- Wear a single strand necklace that passes the bustline. Creating a longer line there will "pretend" lengthen that room.

- Wear an oblong scarf with no fancy knots, twists, or turns. Just let it go around the neck and end in the next room, past the bustline or near the waist.

- Keep details at the shoulders very simple. Don't bring attention here. A shawl lapel on a jacket will visually lengthen this area too.

If this is a long room for your partner, she's got "room to move." Here's what you could advise her to do:

- Wear multiple strands of pearls or necklaces, or bigger, bolder necklaces. She's got the room to do it in.
- Wear scarves wrapped around the neck a few times or tied at the neck, falling down the chest.
- She could wear clothes with a lot of collar detail. She could do that with open collars, with a bright color blouse or top inside a suit.

Where you've got space, flaunt it, show it off, highlight it. It's like showing off your antique Persian rug in your living room where there's room to enjoy it..

Okay, let's move on now to room number two, the area from the underarm to the break of leg. If the area is shorter than others, then you want to do things that will seem like they are lengthening this room. They could include:

- Wearing skirts with facings and not waistbands.
- If you're tucking in a blouse, pull it out a little to create a longer waist.
- If you wear a belt, make it one inch or smaller in width, or wear a hip belt that drops below the waist.
- Elongate this area by dropping the waistline of a dress or jacket. Wear long jackets and/or tunics that bypass the waist.

If you have "room to move" here, this is what you can do:

- Wear clothes with waistband detail—either big waistbands, wide belts or sashes, or other fancy goings on that make the area between the hip and the bust more decorative.
- Wear short-cropped jackets or bolero jackets.
- Use the waist to introduce another color, different from the bottom color. Or wear a dress that has stripes running across it in this area.

Is the number smaller in the third room? If there's not much room there, then:

- Don't wear short skirts. It'll draw attention to the crowded conditions. Go to the knee with your skirt lengths or lower.
- Give up on wearing a skirt that has a lot of detail along the hem if it's ending at the knee. This draws the eye up into that area where you're short.

Are you long in this area? I don't meet a lot of people who are especially long here although I suspect Melanie Griffith is one of them. In the movie *Now and Then* where she's having a reunion with her girlfriends from elementary school (with Rosie O'Donnell, Demi Moore, and Rita Wilson) she's wearing short skirts galore and she looks SO LONG in that room. It helps that she's tall by nature, but tall or short, if you're long here, you can do more things in this area, like this:

- Wear short skirts
- Have detail in this area from the knee and above—this could be trim on a skirt, stripes, sequins, beads—that kind of thing.
- You also can use color in this area to break it up. But if you have a different color in that third room then I still want you to bring it up somehow near your face in an earring or a lipstick so that color repeats near your face and doesn't just hang out alone down there.

If the number is larger in the fourth room, there are a few fun things you can do:

- Wear long skirts, either straight or flowing that end mid-calf or ankle length or floor length.
- Wear capri pants.

- Wear fancy schmancy shoes or boots with detail. Again, if it's a color thing, bring the color back up to your face in a lipstick, a pin, a scarf, or something so your bottom half connects to your top half.

If you are shorter in the fourth room:

- Wear skirts that end at the knee.
- Wear long pants.
- Keep skirt hem, stockings, and shoes in the same tone.

Your body enjoys bringing attention to where it is long. It's likely that you are doing this naturally or intuitively.

So! Good job. Thank your partner and now take a break. When you come back in here, we're going to be working with four-foot-long, thin dowels. I want no play sword fighting with these, so go outside and do some jumping jacks or something. Be back here in ten minutes.

Dowel Work

Okay, class, welcome back. While you were all out having a smoke, Judy asked me a very good question and I'd like to answer it right away. She said, "Why the heck do we have to know this stuff anyway?" Good question. Well, your body wants to feel good in clothes. When God created bodies, He/She created variety. He/She never wanted to create the same thing twice. Maybe God had Attention Deficit Disorder. Anyway, it's up to you to discover which combo God gave you and learn to dress your body so it's happy in clothes.

Okay, we're going to keep using those math skills you learned in high school. Find your partner again and be ready to point out your crotches. You're going to use a pair of four-foot wooden dowels with one-half inch diameter. You can pick these up in bins at the hardware store if you plan to go home and measure your husband's body or other bodies in your neighborhood.

Stand in front of a full-length mirror and hold the dowel horizontally across your crotch area. Have your partner measure the distance from the top of your head to the dowel and then measure from your dowel to the floor. The crotch is what divides your body from your legs. It would be the halfway point between your upper and lower body if you were perfectly proportioned. Remember, God is creative, so don't wig out if you don't see equal numbers.

If your upper half is longer than its lower half, create balance with more illusion. Break up the long space or make it look shorter with horizontal stripes, a belt in the same color as the bottom pant or skirt, a short jacket, a jacket with no cuffs, and lots of attention from the bust up (read the **Bust Up and Put Together** chapter for ideas).

If you are longer in the bottom half it's really not a big deal unless it's grossly out of balance. Neither women nor men consider long legs much of a problem, but if you want to lengthen the torso, here are some ways you can do it visually: Wear hip huggers or go beltless at the waist, or wear prints at the lower half of the body.

Fashion *Fizzyology*

Ready for the next measuring exercise? Get back in front of the mirror. Let your partner line the dowels up along your sides, from the shoulder to your hips on the outside. Look at the lines your body forces these dowels to make. Are the dowels straight up and down indicating a balanced shoulder/hip line, or do the dowels go in or out either at the top or the bottom? If the shoulder is narrower than the hip, the dowels will be going in at the top. If your hips are narrower than your shoulders, the dowels will be going out at the top.

If your shoulders are narrower, you are a candidate for wearing a shoulder pad to bring balance to the hip. Or you can create more visual length at your shoulders and balance your hips by wearing necklines that extend across the shoulders, like the bateau or a boat neck.

If your shoulders are wider than your hips, don't worry about it much. This is another one of those imbalances that doesn't present much of a problem in fashion. If your shoulders are buffed out from training at the gym, you just want fabric and clothes to ease over those muscles, so don't wear things too tight. You'll avoid looking like you have football shoulders, which isn't a bad thing, just a fit thing. Your shoulders will enjoy having some room to move.

What Line Are You Anyway?

Now put those dowels down before you hurt somebody. The last thing we're going to do is look at your inside lines and your outside lines. Stand in front of the mirror again and just look at the outside silhouette of your body. Is there a lot of shoulder definition, waist definition, hip definition? Are those outside lines straight or curvy? Are your legs straight up and down or are they curvy? Make some notes about this. Remember that none of these measurements have anything to do with how much you weigh. It's about proportion and line.

Now, looking at your profile from the side, we're going to look at your inside lines, the lines that form inside your body. Look at the fullness of the bust, abdomen, and bottom. Are you curvy or straight?

If you are curvy, then you want fabrics like knits that will curve with your curves or fabrics that have a soft drape to them that will easily go over those curves, like a jersey knit. Clothes with lots of darts or seams accommodate curves. Bias-cut clothing, where fabric is cut on the diagonal rather than on the straight of grain will have a lot more give also.

If you are straight, then straighter, boxier silhouettes will be happy with your body because they don't have curves and your body doesn't have curves.

There, you know a lot more about how your body hangs together than you did an hour ago. Think back on clothes you wore and wore until they were in shreds. Most likely, they were cut well for your proportions. Think about those things you put on but took off because they didn't "feel" right. They probably weren't well proportioned to your body. Use the info you gathered today next time you're in the dressing room. When you see the pattern of your body, it's easier to be on the lookout for the clothes it likes best.

Let's talk about petites for a minute. A woman who can consider buying clothes in the petite department is 5'4" or shorter. The reason to go there is that the clothes will be proportioned according to her frame. If she tries on a regular jacket and a petite one and they have patch pockets at the hip, they'll actually sit on the right spot in the petite jacket and will be out of reach for her fingertips in the regular jacket. Women look devoured by clothes if they aren't proportioned right.

Now, with our petite woman, although the clothes are scaled to her frame, her personality could be big, big, big. Or her voice could be loud, loud, loud. Or the features of her face could be large, large, large. Or she could have Snow White coloring — dark hair and very fair skin resulting in really high contrast in her coloring. If any of this is true, something about her outfit has to be scaled up to "fit" her. The colors need to be brighter, the buttons larger, her jewelry bigger, the prints need to be bolder or larger.

If you're looking at clothes, think about this for yourself, whether you are petite or not. Have a big personality? Scale up. On the quiet side with soft coloring also? Scale down.

Get your clothes to
look like you.

You don't want to be an imposter.

That's it, Class. Come back next week when we talk about the Deconstruction of the Side Seam and Its Effect on Popular Culture. No one has signed up for it yet, but it's not too late.

Fit First

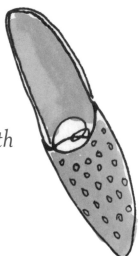

*I want you associating
the fit of your clothes with
the fit of the best kisser
you ever had.*

OOH BABY, TURN THE LIGHTS DOWN LOW, pull out a Marvin
Gaye CD from your collection, and slip it into your CD player. I
want you in the mood when we talk about this sexy subject of fit.
Yes, Baby, I'm talking fit. Good fit, glorious fit. The fit that's right
for you, just the way you like it.

Do I see a quizzical look on your face? Not sure what I'm
talking about? I'm going to move through this real slow. All right,
think about the last good kiss you had in the dark. Everything
connected just right. His lips to yours, his tongue to yours, his
arms around you just right, a perfect fit and a great result.
Win/win, everyone's happy. I want you associating the fit of your
clothes with the fit of the best kisser you ever had. Accept nothing less. Are you with me?

If you don't know this experience of terrific fit, don't be down
on yourself. It can be learned and acquired, though women have a
distinct disadvantage in the fit department. First of all, we have
this thing we trip out on called size (we've been through this now,
haven't we?) where we are never happy with the size we are in so
we put ourselves into sizes we are not and this causes something

called Poor Fit. If that kind of fit were a kiss, it would be a bad kiss. I don't want that for you. I want you to have only good kisses.

Most women don't know good fit because they don't know to expect it. Men have a huge advantage here. They have their clothes tailored for them before they even walk out of the store. They choose a suit or sports coat from a vast selection of sizes that include regular or long, that take into account waist sizes and leg length, neck width and sleeve length. An experienced tailor appears next to the man's dressing room with a trained eye and tailor's chalk ready to mark the suit to perfection. He may take in the waist of the pant or let it out. Men's garments have ample seam allowance so when they put on a few pounds, there's plenty of room on the insides of the garment to make the necessary adjustments. The tailor checks the shoulders, adding extra padding to one side if the shoulder line slopes, taking the jacket in the back if it ripples, adjusting the sleeve length.

Is there a tailor's office right next to the women's dressing rooms? No. Women's garments usually have a narrow seam allowance and most clothes can't be adjusted like men's. Women wrestle with the idea of alterations, mostly because they don't understand them, they aren't used to having them, and they have built-in low self-esteem when it comes to fit. If something doesn't fit them right off the bat, they take it personally. "Something's wrong with me," they quickly surmise. Read this quote: "A man has his clothes made to fit him; a woman makes herself fit her clothes." It's from Edgar Watson Howe. Are you up in arms yet? I want you shouting, "We are not going to do that anymore. We are going to act like men and have clothes made to fit us."

Forget about size. Go for fit. Understand fit. Make "Fit First!" your mantra. I mean to revolutionize your thinking, so you'll put fit first when you're shopping. If it doesn't fit you, you'll either struggle to wear it or you just won't wear it. What's the sense in buying clothes that you don't wear?

So, let's get back to those kisses, your bedroom, and the Marvin Gaye CD.

Doing It in the Dark

I want you to do this in the dark. It's a Fit Feel test. Slip into something from your closet that you love the fit of, that fit-wise is the closest to that best kiss you ever had. Close your eyes and just feel this garment on your body. Do you love the way the bottom graces your hips? Are you thrilled with the way the waistband is soft and narrow and doesn't grab you when you bend over? Try to define what you feel—or if words fail you, just moan with delight. Like a kiss that satisfies, you can recognize the feel of good fit with your eyes closed. Savor this feeling for a good couple of minutes before you move on to the next part of the Fit Feel test.

Ready? Now reach for something in your closet that you've been having trouble with, something that when you put it on, stays on your body for less than two minutes before you're tossing it over a chair and grabbing for something else. Slip it on. Using the "feel" test, take a minute to get a reading on the fit. Are you reaching back to grab the extra bulk of fabric gathering under the arms? Does it feel sloppy? Too big in places? Or is it too tight in places? Are you tugging at the midriff area of the top trying to get more room there? Is your waistband pinching? When you sit down do you get a prairie dog mound of fabric in your lap? Is your collar hugging your neck comfortably, or do you keep yanking it forward? Are your sleeves too long or too short? Now that you're curious about all of this, open your eyes and look in the mirror and see if you can see what's not fitting you properly.

Most of the things that don't fit us correctly could be identified, discussed, and maybe even remedied if we knew to expect great fit. It would be like in the old days, say pre-1900 when dressmakers would go from town to town designing and fitting clothes for whole families. There were no ready-made clothes. Dressmakers created patterns and fabric was chosen. Clothes were made up according to each person's particular body shape and imperfections. Then the clothes were delivered and they fit, perfectly. That's a custom-made wardrobe.

If you had your own dressmaker, she would know everything about your body and she would design fit to be perfect. The collar of your blouse would hug your neck and stay there—not too tight and not too loose. The curves of a jacket would follow your curves—your waist, your hips—and rest just alongside them. When you buttoned your jacket, the buttons and buttonholes would line up. Nothing would gap or pull. If there were pockets in your jacket or in your pants, your hands would slip naturally into them.

Most of us deal in ready-made clothes, so we have to be prepared to recognize good fit and demand it if it's missing. If you took the "feel" test in the dressing room (or at home while you still had the tags on so you could take the garment back if you wanted to), you would have made the first step in determining fit. Is it comfortable? Do you feel at ease in your body?

Think *Fit* First

With your eyes open, it's so easy to be influenced by the color, the pattern, the texture of the fabric or the function of the garment. There are reasons staring you in the face that keep you from thinking fit first. With your eyes open, you may make a deal with fit. You stare at yourself in the mirror and say, "I love these pants! The color, the weight of them, they're perfect. But tight. Well, if I lose those five pounds I've been wanting to lose, it'll fit okay."

Stop right there, Missy. Forget about the five pounds. I want these clothes to be in your closet this week for you to enjoy. If you lose those five pounds, we'll deal with the alterations later. For now, it's fit first just the way you are.

I want everything fitting you properly so when that yummy kiss comes around, you are thinking only about those lips on yours, and not the waistband that's pinching you.

Now I want you to look at good fit with your eyes open. This is how Helena Chenn, a dressmaker and an alteration expert, defines good fit: "Whereas quality is quantifiable (the number of carats in a diamond, the year of a vintage), fit is a pure sensation. When you see good fit, it is characterized by a garment that follows the shape of the body with no indications of stress or wrinkling. The shoulder seam sits on top of the shoulder. The curves at the neckline, armholes, hips, and waistline follow the natural contours of the body without binding or gapping. The length of the sleeves and hems are smooth and even around the entire width of the garment and falls at the most flattering point on the woman. If you relax, drop your shoulders, straighten your spine, and sigh with ease, chances are you're experiencing good fit."

Wow! What a concept! I know this is new to lots of you. We're just used to bad fit. I want to change all that. I want you seeing yourself in that dressing room with an alterations person checking you over just like the guys have their tailors. The sleeves of your blouse have been checked so they aren't too long or too short. The hem on your skirt is even all around (even if it's a bias-cut skirt!). When you close your jacket, there is no pulling at the buttonholes. The shoulder of the jacket follows your shoulder line, and doesn't slip over it.

Great fit and great kisses are a lot alike. Great fit and great kisses are ones you want to come back to over and over again. Christie, my writing buddy, told me about the great pants she bought. She was ecstatic. She said, "The butt, the crotch, the waist . . . it was all perfect! All I want to do is wear these pants that fit. Since I got them, I went into my closet and threw all those pants away that don't fit me right. Now I know how pants should fit."

It's like that kiss, isn't it? A great one is so memorable and that sets the standard. I hope you have something in your closet that sets the standard for good fit, something you can measure other decisions by.

The New Frontier

Lycra added to cotton, linen, silk, or other blends of fabrics has created a new frontier when it comes to fit. Because of that small percentage of added Lycra to the fiber content, clothes have a natural give. More styles are available to you than before because Lycra gives you leeway in fit. Maybe you didn't think you could wear close-fitting silhouettes because of the strain at the shoulder area or back of the arms. Now you can! More Lycra means more possibilities.

Fit is very personal. Someone might tell you there's a standard for something, but if it's not your standard, forget it. I can bet that how one person wants to be kissed may not be the way another person wants to be kissed. **It's personal. You just have to know what you like.**

In this regard, "style" more than anything can influence fit. You'll notice that the more fashion-forward a woman is (on the cutting edge of fashion trends), the longer her pant legs are, creating more of a break in them, which requires a longer hem. Same with her sleeve length. Although a sleeve length technically is measured five and a half inches from the tip of your thumb, you may like a longer, more exaggerated look and therefore style is going to dictate how you alter that sleeve. People really into fashion would consider themselves fashion-forward and tend to wear things longer. A conservative person would probably be really uncomfortable with this. Here again, know who you are.

When I'm in the dressing room with you, I'm watching you. If you're pulling, yanking, or tugging, we've got problems with fit and usually I'm running out and pulling another size. If it's slipping or sliding a bit, I'm going to study it in the mirror and do some fiddling with it until I get it looking just right. I'll use some pins to hold it in place so you can see how it should look. If you're satisfied, then we'll bring in the alterations person and have her mark it for you.

When I'm in the dressing room with you, I'm listening for which fit works for you. What feels tight to one person is nearly loose to someone else. Sherry likes to add a gusset in the crotch of her pants to give her more room down there. She sits all day in her job and she wants to feel completely comfortable. This would drive someone else crazy who would be feeling like she was in droopy drawers with all that extra fabric down there. It's okay to stay true to yourself. If something bugs you and you know how to eliminate that irritation even if it isn't visible to anyone else, go for it. Often there are standard things that we learn about ourselves that we can pass on to an alterations person. One leg is longer, one hip is higher than the other, one shoulder drops lower than the other one. I'm short waisted I want all waistbands off, one thigh area is curvier than the other and I need the thinner side to be taken in so it lies smooth. It's very common to have little things that need consistent attention. These are all things you look for each time in good fit. Good for you.

Good fit makes us do things we wouldn't normally do. "I'm buying three of these," a client will say when she comes across a great fitting jean, as hard to find as a good kisser with a steady income. When you can identify what good fit is, you will know a pot of gold when you see one and buy smart, like she did.

Fit is Good

Now, if you're a woman, you know that your body changes during the month, and sometimes this means your clothes fit differently throughout the month. Allow for that. Maybe there's a week out of the month that a certain pant doesn't fit you well. Wear something else during that time, but beyond that, if you have a bunch of clothes in your closet that aren't fitting you properly and haven't for a long time, do something about it. They create dead space if those clothes aren't useful to you. Either alter them, or it's out, out, out, get them out. Realize that if it's a weight thing, a loss of thirty-five pounds will leave something pretty much impossible to alter and you need to buy new clothes.

There's so much pleasure to be had from learning what good fit is and going for it. I want you enjoying the way that blouse feels over your torso, the way the pants feel at your waist and hips, the way the hem of them comes down perfectly in line with your cute shoe. When you love the way you look, and love the feel of how you look, it makes a big difference in who you kiss and how good those kisses are. Besides, the last thing I want you to be thinking about while in that hot embrace is how uncomfortable your pants are. You may be tempted to take them off way before you should.

Take your clothes off **for all the right reasons,** not for a lame one, like your clothes don't fit right.

Wedgies and Other Misfits

Your wardrobe is a
fine-tuned machine.
Like your car, it needs check-ups
and adjustments to keep it purring.

AH, SINCE WE WERE TOGETHER IN THE LAST CHAPTER, you've been moaning in delight over good fit, either from feeling it on your body or imagining it in your rich mind. And you've got an understanding of your body, whether it likes to be fitted into curves because you're curvy, or it enjoys straight lines because of your straight lines. You know (because you measured) where you are short and where you are long, so you have fewer questions about where the prime location is for your skirt hem to hang. You've come a long way, Baby!

Ready to go for some extra credit in Fit Class? We'll reinforce what good fit looks like by looking at misfits. You've seen these yourself. They're easy to spot from a bench in the center of a mall. Come with me. Let's do some people watching.

Two women in jeans go by and the way those jeans fit from the back, they look like they're man-made wedgie producers. Remember guys in high school who loved giving wedgies to other guys—pulling their pants up in back so the seam goes where thong underwear hangs out? You can imagine how uncomfortable that must be. Yet these women are wearing their jeans like that with no help from a mean-spirited high schooler. Why?

To get the straight scoop on why these jeans are producing wedgies when they fit fine everywhere else, we've got Helena Chenn with us again today. As I mentioned in the last chapter, Helena is a custom dressmaker. She makes clothes from scratch as well as alters existing clothes bought ready-made, even jeans. "Why do some jeans do that, Helena?"

She says, "When they cut jeans, they cut that back seam so it'll fit close to the body. But that wedgie look is cutting it too close."

Wedgies are not fashionable, people. They're distracting. If this is happening to you, try different styles. Traditional cut jeans are for the tall and lean body. In this pant, legs are straight, hips are straight. The reverse cut jean accommodates a smaller waist and is wider at the hips. The relaxed fit is cut a full two inches fuller in the hip and thigh area with a slight taper to the ankle. Can you tell from these descriptions what shape you should be looking for? Fashion is generous. It's here to serve you. It offers choices. Keep looking until you find the jean that fits your shape.

Here's a symptom of another pant misfit. It's those stacked wrinkles that show up in lines like kitty-cat whiskers on either side of the crotch area in the front of pants.

Helena, our expert explains why this happens.

She says, "If you're getting wrinkles there, then the crotch isn't long enough. You need more room in the crotch depth. If a woman has a tummy, it will be taking up some of that room and she'll need either a larger size or a different style that is cut longer there."

The Long and the Short of It

Aha! This brings up a term you all should know: "rises." We talk about short rises and long rises. The rise is the distance from your crotch to your waist. Often you can get the right rise for your body by shopping in the right department.

Here's how. Junior brands are cut for a younger body. Their clothes are cut smaller and tighter. If you have a grown up body and you've been trying to shop in the junior department of major department stores, be kind to yourself and head for the departments where clothes are cut bigger and longer. Fit relief could just be a few feet away in the women's department.

Here's another pant scenario. I've seen this happen when women are trying on a pant and I ask them to sit down in a chair to see how comfortable it is. As they settle into the seat, fabric rises up in their lap like a prairie dog mound.

"Try a different style," our expert says, "They need a pant that's cut with a shorter rise."

Pants that have Lycra in them, even just one percent, naturally give more ease in the fabric, so if fit is problematic in the rise, this can be a solution. A little bit of lycra makes the fabric softer. Jeans made with lycra are far more comfortable because those inside seams are softer.

While we have the expert fitter here, let's ask her what to expect when a tailor goes about fitting clothes. Pay attention because this is what you should expect when you have your own clothes tailored. Helena says, "A general rule is to fit from the top down. On a blouse, dress, or jacket, always check and pin the collar area first. Then proceed to the shoulders, sides, and last of all the length of sleeves or hem. With pants, always check and pin the waist and side first before proceeding to the hem. Any alteration done to the body of a garment will affect the length, so it must be pinned first. Sometimes you will have to sew the alteration in the body first and come back for a second fitting for the length."

So if you are in a dressing room without me or Helena, expect a fitter to go through those steps. Ask questions, pay attention. **They know their stuff.**

Although a fitter can really fine-tune a garment to fit your body, there are some things that you just have to give up on. You cannot change the line of a garment from one design to another, such as from a dolman sleeve to a set-in sleeve. If there's been a weight loss of thirty-five pounds or more, give up on the alterations and buy something new.

Fit All Over

Here is a short list of things that can be altered so you're not in a misfit. Starting from the top, shoulders can be brought in and made narrower. Bringing a shoulder in just one inch can make a significant difference and is worth it. If you're wider at the hip, you're buying a bigger size to give ease over the hip area; that means your shoulders aren't filling that shoulder line in, so it's collapsing and that doesn't look good. Have it pulled in a bit so it rests naturally on your shoulder. Don't worry about balancing your hips. We can add more attention to the shoulder and face area to balance a bigger hip.

I can hear you now. "But, Bren, I never button my jackets." I don't care. Be able to button it even if you don't plan to. Buy the size that fits the biggest part of your body and make adjustments from there.

If a collar is sitting away from the neck, it too can be brought in closer for a better fit.

Lapels on a jacket can be narrowed, something I recommend if you have a narrow face. Wide lapels can drown out a petite face. A wide face loves wide lapels. They get along very well.

If a jacket is boxy and you are curvy and you want that jacket to follow your curves, it can be brought in. A curvy jacket cannot be made boxy.

Your clothes wear you instead of you wearing your clothes if there is too much extra fabric or bulk. So look carefully at the back. Is there extra fabric that could be taken out, leaving the garment trimmer so you look trimmer too? Also on the sleeves of a jacket, narrowing them is another way of removing bulk. Removing bulk leaves you looking slimmer, something some women keep insisting on.

Sleeve length, of course, can be altered and should be. The standard is to measure from the tip of the thumb to your wrist, approximately five and a half inches.

You can take a waistband off of a slack if it is crowding you. If you are long in the torso, you do not have this issue. If you are uncomfortable with waistbands that measure more than half an inch, consider having it taken off completely. Comfort is key!

Because of the lack of adequate seam allowance in most women's clothes, waistbands (and other seams) cannot usually be let out, so again, start with the size that fits the widest part of you. Don't buy a pant with a tight waistband. You will be unhappy all day, which is not what I want for you.

A skinny pant needs a shorter hem or you can't slip it over your foot. Wider pants can have a longer hem (creating a bigger break) which will sit further out on your shoe.

If you're in the dressing room and the store has an alterations expert, have that expert summoned to take a look at all the important points of the outfit, from shoulders to the bottom hem of the skirt or pant or coat. Fine adjustments make a dramatic difference.

Make friends with your own "Helena." Every woman should have a good alterations person on speed dial. Find someone in your area who understands how to fit your clothes to your body. Your wardrobe is a fine-tuned machine. Like your car, it needs check-ups and adjustments to keep it purring. This person will learn your body's roadmap and keep you from wedgies or other misfits.

You're **worth** it, Baby.

Bust Up and Put Together

*Looking at a woman
who is put together is like
looking at a beautiful painting.*

ALL RIGHT, I'M GOING TO BE STRAIGHT WITH YOU. I want you to be able to look put together every single day, whether you are in your sweats in exercise class, dressed for work, going out on a date, or going to a lecture hall to hear a speaker. I want people talking behind your back — "Gee, she looks *so* put together." In fact, I want you to have a reputation for looking put together.

Why am I so adamant about this? It's because I know how the world works, and when you are visible (as you are when you look put together), you get things like good service or being noticed when your boss is looking to make promotions in the department. People who are put together just seem luckier in life and I believe it's because they are visible. They stand out. Their put together look sends out nonverbal messages of respect, honor, intention. It's the difference between having people look at you and see you in focus rather than out of focus. Let people see how great you are. Don't hide behind a messy, disheveled look.

Look sharp! Be sharp!

It's unfortunate, but people who don't look put together often get overlooked. They go unnoticed. They are easier to ignore, easier to be disrespectful to. Hey, I wish it wasn't so. People read other people's appearances and make judgements about it without even trying. I want people to be making the best possible judgements about you. I want you to stand out—in a good way. Women who are put together look smart, sharp, respectable, with it, and not someone who could be pushed around or ignored.

Okay, so that's how I see it. Now, as to the mechanics of looking put together, let me tell you that it *is* possible. You may be one of the skeptics out there who appreciates a put together woman, but thinks it's just too hard to achieve, so won't even try. Maybe you think it's for geniuses, naturals, talented-from-birth types. Not true. Not true at all. It takes some learning, some practicing, some discipline, but you can do it. I have faith in you!

Put together comes from many sources. I'm going to demonstrate it every way I can so that you'll look at your clothes, put things together, and look put together as naturally as you tear up at a movie when the two lovers realize they really were meant for each other despite their obstacles.

Hey, there it is! I'll try to get all the obstacles out of the way. When I break this down for you, you'll see how easy it is to be put together in all parts of your life. You're going to fall in love with how you look.

What's It
All About?

Let's agree on what put together looks like. Looking at a woman who is put together is like looking at a beautiful painting. Something about how she looks draws you in — maybe it's a hit of color under her jacket, or a lovely necklace at her neck, the contrast of her striking face and haircut with her uncluttered clothing — so you can't help yourself from noticing her beauty. Once you've been drawn in by that focal point, your eye moves across the canvas of her ensemble, noticing little things along the way, such as how she repeats an accent color — a pumpkin-colored silk blouse, a pumpkin-colored leather handbag resting on her shoulder. Maybe she opts to wear clothes in her own coloring — wearing a color in her eyes, her skin, her hair. Maybe she accentuates a line — repeating the line of her necklace with the second line of her scooped top. Or she repeats a texture by wearing a belt in the same shiny smooth leather as her shoes. Maybe it's a woman wearing an eggplant suit with a bold geometric, colorful blouse and then wearing a thin sock that is also geometric and colorful, but smaller in scale than the blouse. Art elements — line, color, or texture — and the repetition of them draws your eye through a whole painting, or an ensemble, leaving you satiated and pleased like a well presented and prepared meal.

There are all kinds of art. There's impressionistic art, soft and blending, like an ash-blond woman with green-gray eyes dressed in soft pastel-colored knits, which are dreamy and easy on the eye. There's pop art, the Andy Warhol-type, that grabs your eye and holds it, like a woman using color blocking—a lime-green shirt, black skirt, a red scarf at her neck and blocky, chunky jewelry—modern and punchy. There are formal, quiet portraits by Rembrandt who was commissioned to paint portraits of aristocrats. This could be likened to a woman wearing classic clothes, nothing funky or arty, more refined things in smooth fabrics, modest silhouettes, fine jewelry.

Put together is:

- staying true to the elements of a painting style.
- telling a story clearly, concisely, with no more detail than is needed to get the clear picture.
- keeping your story straight. It's wearing a relaxed shoe with a relaxed pant, a dressy shoe with a dressy dress.
- in the little things—buying an umbrella and thinking about what color umbrella will be most pleasing with your raincoat.
- wearing clothes organically in the season they were made for—linen in summer, corduroy in fall. The same way that you enjoy fruits and vegetables at the peak of their season— acorn squash in the fall, strawberries in the summer—wear the colors and fabrics that fit the season you're in: rich autumn-colored clothes in autumn, shaded and darker clothes in winter, light clothes and bright colors in the summer when the sun is brightest.

The Bust Up Review

Got the picture? Now let's get started on some "how-to's." I'm going to make this easy for you by breaking this big idea into parts. Instead of tackling being put together from head-to-toe,

I'm going to start off first from the bust on up to your face. I'll connect your legs and belly later.

There's a lot of impact to be made from the bust up. First of all, in most legitimate businesses, you want your audience to have their attention heading up to your face, your communication center. There are professions that focus say, from the waist down, but that's a different book.

Mostly, if you're meeting people from behind your desk, they are seeing you from the bust up. If you're at a podium giving a speech, they are seeing you from the bust up. If you're selling wares from behind a counter, you're seen from the bust up. If you're having dinner with a new love interest, you're sitting across the table from each other and what is he looking at? Your bust up. Let's make it important, dynamic. Let's make it picture perfect.

Come with me. We're going to the photographer's studio where you're getting a new headshot taken. This really forces you to think of the bust up. Persia, my makeup artist, will do your hair and makeup. She'll use some hot rollers or some gel, mousse, or wax to make your hair look healthy and pretty around your face. She'll define those eyebrows of yours, make a good clean eyebrow line, fill them in if they are fading, thin them out if they're too thick. She'll apply makeup on your face so you look polished, finished, inviting.

The photographer, Sandy, has asked you to bring a few outfits. She looks for the one that gives the most contrast so you will show up clearly. She asks you to wear your shiny gold earrings rather than matte ones. She doesn't want anything to look cluttered on you, so she removes the pin you're wearing and just goes with the necklace and earrings. You sit on the stool in front of the backdrop. Sandy smoothes your jacket across your shoulders, brushes your shoulders in case there are any dandruff flakes resting there.

Snap, snap, snap goes the shutter of the camera. A week later you look at the proofs and they are mind-blowingly wonderful. So how do we do this in real life outside of the studio? You follow the map that Persia and Sandy laid out for you, starting with paying attention to your grooming. Here's your put together checklist for your face:

1. Keep your haircut current and your hair coloring current as well. Be sure the color and cut flatter your face and your natural coloring.

2. Keep those eyebrows groomed—tweezed, dyed, or filled in with color. They are framing your face, Girls.

3. Wear makeup. Just a little bit adds polish to your face. A face that has makeup on makes the features of the face stand out more and be distinctive. Learn something new about makeup every six months. Update colors. A great new face of color and design can inspire a whole new life!

4. Eyewear is important. If you haven't changed your frames in a couple of years, you're making a date with me to go to the eyewear boutique and shop for new glasses. If your hair has changed colors, getting new glasses jumps to the top of your to-do list. Get a frame that incorporates some aspect of your own coloring—either in your face, your eyes, or your hair. Gold frames are harsh with gray hair. Shiny finishes are harsher on an older face. Ask for nonglare coating on your lenses so we can see your pretty eyes without any glare.

5. Even though your hand may not have been in that photograph, tend to your nails. Manicures are a must. Clean,

groomed nails mean you care about yourself and you take care of yourself. Pass that message on.

Okay, with the face finished, let me show you some good bust up shots. I want you to look at these shots as if you were holding up a big beautiful picture frame and the bust and up is sitting inside that picture frame. Take a close look.

Picture this: A red-headed woman wears solid colored clothes and then adds a scarf in a rust color that repeats her hair color. The scarf has connected her head to her shoulders.

Picture this: Wearing high contrast (especially if your coloring is high contrast) is like wearing an explanation point. A near-black haired woman with fair skin wears a zebra print top and you can't take your eyes off her face.

Picture this: A blond-haired woman wears a light, golden leather jacket. The metallic finish in the jacket is picked up in the highlights of her blond hair.

Picture this: One way to bring attention to your face is to introduce a dynamic color inside a jacket. With a black jacket, use a bright color for contrast — orange, lime green, lemon yellow.

Picture this: A woman with green eyes wears an eyeglass frame that picks up that same green color of her eye. The frames sit just above her cheekbone and extend just slightly (think cat-eye shape) right by the corner of her eye so *your* eye goes right to her eyes and enjoys the lovely resonance of color. She's wearing a white blouse and has a green (you guessed it! the same as her eyes!) shawl over one shoulder.

Picture this: A necklace falls in the same shape as the shape of the top you're wearing. A V-neck sweater with a pendant that drops in the same V-line works great. A scoopneck sweater with a more rounded necklace repeats the curved line.

Don't do this: Whippy necklaces, those thin gold chains, rarely add up to anything in a put together look. Shop for something more stunning, more substantial. Trade all those thin things in for something chunkier, relating to whatever scale your features are. Big-scale features (large nose, big eyes or full Julia Roberts-type mouth) need big-scale jewelry. Small delicate features (small eyes, tiny nose, thin lips) need delicate, smaller pieces of jewelry. Combination features (big nose, thin lips) can choose or combine scale in earrings and necklace. This could look like a chunky corded metal necklace. The size is large scale; the lines formed by the cording are fine lines and give you the smaller scale that comes from the small lips.

The *Cheek* Bone is Connected to the *Leg* Bone

Okay, now, we've got your face and your bust looking sharp. Let's connect the belly and your legs. Let me say this right now. Only if you have just had foot surgery are you allowed to wear tennis shoes with your nice clothes. I mean it.

The way you connect your legs is that you wear a shoe that relates somehow to your outfit—in color, in texture, in personality. And if you're wearing a belt, make the color and texture similar to the shoe. It will automatically draw the eye up the body, moving the eye through the canvas of your beautiful work of art.

I've Seen the *Light*

Now I want to explain something to you that will make you so happy. It will be one of those common sense kinds of things that will practically part the Red Sea of the wardrobe world.

Put together connects the inside and the outside. It does this with color like you saw in some of the snapshots above when we linked people's personal coloring with the color of their clothes. It does it in personality style. A very formal person is not going to wear a prairie skirt. Likewise, an informal person is not going to wear a neat and tidy two-piece suit. Do you see yourself as a formal person or an informal person? Are you the relaxed jeans-type of person or do you like to be suited up, or are you somewhere in between?

Trouble brews in closets when you want to wear an outfit that requires a black shoe to pull it together and the only one you have is the black satin pump. You put it with your jeans and you've struck out. Satin pumps don't go with jeans. It's not a put together look. And there's going to be an easy way to understand this in a minute.

We all know that jeans are not created equally. There's a range from the most casual, working jean, a 501 Levi jean to an elegant jean, for example, a velvet pant with jean styling that you might wear to a dinner party. So if we saw that casual jean and the dressy one on a horizontal line, the casual being the far left edge of the line and the velvet jean being on the far right edge of that line, what we would find in-between, midway, could be a jean from a woman's department in a nice department store, cut for a woman's body, smoother and leaner.

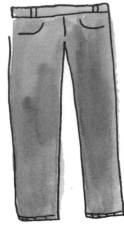

Using these three jeans, we're going to build three outfits—a casual, informal outfit, a dressy outfit, and one in-between.

Let's add a top with those jeans. Imagine that you are placing these **tops** on that line above.

Casual: five-pocket, classic 501 Levi's jeans; brown and green plaid flannel shirt

In-between: Dana Buchman stretch jeans (smoother and leaner); red cotton/Lycra blend scoopneck T-shirt

Dressy: St. John velvet jeans; ivory silk charmeuse blouse with pearl buttons

Now let's add the **shoes.**

Casual: fifteen-year old cowboy boots

In-between: black ankle boots with side zipper

Dressy: black satin sandal

Let's add **accessories**.

Casual: brown, thick, wide belt; brown woven watch; no earrings; worn, large, floppy tote bag

In-between: no belt; stainless steel watch; silver hoop earrings and an Indian silver-and-turquoise bracelet; medium-sized black leather shoulder bag

Dressy: thin, gold, low-slung hip belt; fine, gold small

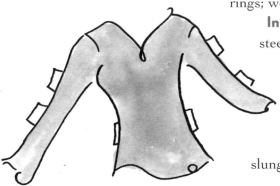

faced dress watch; small gold button earrings; small evening shoulder bag in black satin

You have made three outfits and they are three looks. Now imagine taking parts of the outfit with the dressy jean and putting it with the casual jean. Or vice versa. Those strappy dressy sandals don't work with those 501s and the cowboy boots do not work with the velvet jean.

Outfits
Divided by Three

Here's the Parting-of-the-Red-Sea rule. It parts three ways. Neighboring categories can cohabitate. You can mix elements of the in-between category with the dressy one or the casual one, but you can't mix the clothes that exist on either end. It just doesn't work visually. This alone will have you putting things together in a pleasing way with little effort. When you follow this chart, you won't make the mistake of teaming a rugged outdoorsy sweater with evening pants (I've seen it!). You'll get dressed and walk out of the door confident that no one will think you got dressed this morning in the dark. Copy the chart that follows and put it on the wall of your closet as reference if you need reminders.

The chart below gives you more details about what these categories look like. If you don't understand some of the terms, go to a fabric store and ask a clerk to show you, for example, a damask fabric, cotton jersey knit, a superfine wool. Feel them. Or ask your favorite gay guy. My gay friends have advanced knowledge of fabric and can talk about it with me for hours. If you are lucky enough to have friends like that, put yourself in their capable hands for the lowdown on fabric discrimination.

Here now, is the chart:

	INFORMAL	**IN-BETWEEN**	**FORMAL**
DESCRIPTION	Rugged, rustic, outdoorsy	Relaxed and comfortable, some detailing or fabric interest	Refined, sophisticated, conservative, rich look
COLOR	Lots of earth tones–brown, khaki, camel, natural-colored wools and cottons	Full range of color–plum, cranberry, greens and blues, white, black, navy, aquas, soft yellow	Neutrals–taupe, ivory, gray, medium blues, navy; complex colors, grayed or shaded tones
TEXTURE, FABRICS	Bulky, heavy fabrics like wide-wale corduroy, nappy suede, heavy tweeds, coarse cotton, thick woo, thick denim	Medium-weight cotton, wool, and silk; jersey and cotton knits; fine corduroys	Luxury fabrics like silk, superfine wool, cashmere, satin, smooth fine cottons
LINE	Thick cableknits, thick stripes	Curves, soft diagonals	Nothing complicated, simple and classic silhouettes
PATTERN	Plaids, large scale prints	Medium-scaled prints and stripes, abstracts and geometrics	Pattern on pattern with no color change as in damasks and jacquards; small, even, symmetrical prints
DETAILS	Patch pockets, large buttons, elbow patches, epaulets	Tortoise or pewter buttons, some topstitching, plackets	Covered buttons, no topstitching, no clutter

I've thrown a lot at you—lists, charts, ideas, lots of instruction. Hopefully, it hasn't overwhelmed you. If too many charts send you into back-to-school nightmares, wait! Relax. You're not being tested on any of this. Rather, I hope these details have created some ease for you and your life in clothes. That's my intention. When you're wondering—can I put this denim fanny pack with this silk satin pantsuit?—instead of having a hunch that it wouldn't work, but not following your hunch, now you have clearer boundaries about what to put with what—and you'll follow through with confidence.

Here's your homework, if you choose to do it. Read this chapter over a few times. There's a lot of information to absorb. Once you understand these formulas, rules, and ideas, you'll start people watching and be able to see what works and why, and what doesn't and why. Sit in a quiet garden and contemplate these things. Take a magazine with you and study the fashion pages and see if you can find examples of someone looking really put together.

Although I've broken it down as best I can, remember that there is not one exact recipe to follow. It's a lot of things. Be surprised, be delighted by how someone puts themself together. It will evolve—just like a home's interior will evolve or a menu in a fine restaurant will evolve—so will how you put yourself together. What it looks like today could be very different from how it looks two years from now.

It's not a **static** process.
It's very *organic* and *creative.*
So have *fun* creating your
put together look. I know you're
going to become
famous for it.

Going to Work and What the Heck is Casual Anyway?

This business casual stuff has been as clear as lyrics to rap music—that is, not very clear at all.

I HAVE AN IDEA WHERE "BUSINESS CASUAL" CAME FROM. It's part of a conspiracy theory, but I'm keeping the details to myself. I think conspiracy fanatics are lunatics and ought to be on medication. I don't want to think I've become one of "them," so I'm keeping my mouth shut about it. But I'm not keeping quiet about my opinions on the matter. This business casual stuff has been as clear as lyrics to rap music, that is, not very clear at all. It's so confusing in fact, that you just want to blame this whole thing on someone. You probably have a conspiracy theory too! Work clothes used to be the one area of wardrobe life that people got right. Well, some people did. But business casual is a wardrobe earthquake that has left the workplace in shambles. Let's get some things straight before you shoot yourself in your open-toed-sandaled foot and get yourself reprimanded, demoted, or fired.

"Business casual" sounds like an oxymoron. People hear that term, "business casual," and they hear the "casual" part, not the "business" part. Casual, they think. Okay that means my holey jeans, my favorite (and worn) pink tie-dye T-shirt, and my jean jacket. No, I don't think so.

Then you have problems like this. Jennifer goes to a job interview at a dot-com business. She's dressed in her navy-blue interview skirt suit, hose, and heels. She shows up and sits across from a guy in khakis and feels totally out of place. And he's having a hard time getting past the fact that *she* looks totally out of place in his workplace. He doesn't see her qualifications because he can't get past what she looks like.

It's not his fault. We all read how someone looks and it gives us an impression that's hard to shake—even with an impeccable resume staring us in the face.

I've thought about this for a long time. Do I just give you some quickie answers or do I teach you how to figure this thing out on your own? Do I give you the fish or teach you how to fish? I've decided to teach you how to fish for some great outfits by giving you tools to understand the language of clothes. I want you to be prepared and appropriate so you can do what I always want for you—forget about your clothes. If you show up in what you've calculated to be your best guesstimate, you will be relaxed and comfortable.

Let's Go to Work

Work is a big part of most people's lives. I spend lots of time in dressing rooms helping women get ready to go to work, all kinds of work—doctors, lawyers, managers, entrepreneurs, florists, financial planners, homemakers, teachers, health practitioners, speakers, therapists, graphic designers, singers, actresses, real estate agents, writers, mediators, bankers, trainers, speakers, and more. When I ask each person how they want to be perceived in their work the answers usually include these words: competent, confident, approachable, smart, trustworthy—things like that. They want to look professional. In fact, not a single person I've asked has said, "Gee, I want to confuse the person who's paying me, keep them guessing, make them wonder if they really chose the right person."

Which is exactly what does happen if you don't reinforce your professionalism by demonstrating professional messages in your dress. Take this situation. Pam, a mom of three, had to find a doctor and find one quick. Their family doctor moved to Germany, and she hadn't bothered to find one to take his place. But now her youngest daughter had a fever, couldn't swallow, everything was swollen. Pam called around, got a referral, and the woman doctor was able to fit her daughter in that day. Pam and her daughter arrived at the office, filled out the paperwork, and then were admitted to the doctor's office. The woman doctor, in her late thirties, was wearing a short-sleeved shirt with a pattern that looked like the finale of a Fourth of July fireworks display, blasts of bright colors moving in all directions. This cotton shirt was tucked inside a bagged-out cotton black knit pant with an elastic waistband showing—toddler pull-on-looking pants sized up for big people. She wore plastic earrings with moving parts, like a mobile and in bright colors to match the shirt. She had on bright blue eyeshadow, hot pink lipstick. The back of her head looked like bed head, the way your hair looks when you get up in the morning before you shower. She had white tennis shoes on.

While Pam's daughter was being examined on the examining table, Pam looked all over the room for evidence that this woman really was a doctor. She searched for clues—medical journals, shelves with reference books, framed licenses. Nothing about the woman's appearance gave Pam any peace of mind that she was legitimate. Pam's attention was focused on trying to connect the woman's credentials with her presence. It wasn't computing.

Was she wearing goofy clothes because she was a pediatric doctor trying to put kids at ease? No, she wasn't. She was a doctor for big people. The doctor made a diagnosis, prescribed medicine, and Pam's daughter got better. Did they go back? No, Pam found someone else. It was **impossible** to link **confidence** and **competence** with someone who looked like she might be a **nursery school aide,** not someone who'd been through **years of medical school.**

When someone's appearance doesn't match his or her professional stature, we're distracted. We can't focus. We look for visual proof of credentials. If someone doesn't look like they are taking their job seriously, we seriously do not want to give them our business. In business, you want clothes to be appropriate so they can disappear and be a nonissue.

So, since you all want to look professional in your professional lives, I am going to give you the clothing symbols—color, fabrics, texture, line, pattern, detail, and fit—to translate your desires into work outfits. This "symbol" breakdown comes to you courtesy of Cheryl Birch, former image consultant. You won't believe how easy this makes getting dressed. It's a lot like those paint by number kits you had as a kid. You can look like a pro, instantly.

Color Your World

Color has inherent messages. Color sends out meaning like signals from a radio tower. It is the strongest communicator of all the symbols in clothing. It affects us physically, mentally, and emotionally. High intensity colors are exciting—hot pink, bright orange, watermelon red—but they will tire an audience over time. It's not a color you want to be wearing as a seminar leader for an all-day course. On the other hand, low intensity, neutral colors are easy to be with for long periods of time—camel, cream, soft gray, taupe—would be effortless to be with all day. That's why "neutrals" are so common in business. They're easy to be around.

Intense color makes you memorable. That's why wearing a small amount of it is prudent in business. The higher the contrast in color, the more authority is the message that's sent out—the lower the contrast, the lower the authority level. So if you're in a situation that you want a lot of authority in, say a high school principal, charcoal gray and white will give it to you where baby blue and pale yellow won't.

We respond to color automatically. We can't help ourselves. We've all experienced the effect of color, whether it's a man in a dark suit, a woman in red, or a toddler in baby blue. When we encounter others in living color, their choices send a resounding message. Are you sending the message you intend? I am giving you a color shortcut. Here is my list of colors and the meaning or emotional tone I associate with each of them. When you wear these colors you communicate these values. When we see colors, we expect the people to be the same way. It's hard to convince us differently. Ready? Here it is.

NAVY honesty, integrity, trustworthy, hardworking, organized

BLACK sophisticated, high authority, power, assertive, mysterious, sensual

WHITE fresh, clean, hopeful, reliable, artistic, expressive

TAN/CREAM/CAMEL elegant, approachable, nonoffensive, trusting

BROWN stable, secure, persevering, slow to change

RUST earthy, friendly, approachable

CHARCOAL GRAY strength of character, authoritative, refined

BURGANDY/MAROON classic, refined, elegant, formal

PLUM regal, diplomatic, sophisticated

TEAL inventive, soothing, balancing

INDIGO (DARK-BLUE VIOLET) creative, unusual, artistic, intuitive

RED dramatic, self-assured, active, high energy, courageous

ORANGE social, fun loving, enthusiastic, thoughtful

YELLOW creative, outgoing, bright, cheerful, optimistic

GREEN nurturing, friendly, kind, peaceful, helpful

BLUE communicator, logical, thinking, soothing, inspiring, honest, approaches new ideas more conservatively, dedicated to high ideals

VIOLET sensitive, unusual, psychic, spiritual, exotic, has strong sense of inner self and life direction

PINK quiet, refined, artistic, universal color of love, will exhibit lasting devotion to people, places, and ideals

CORAL combination of pink and orange attributes

LAVENDER usually a person searching for their life direction, can be devoted, humble, shy

TURQUOISE/AQUA combination of green and blue attributes, kind, soothing, friendly, bright-more outgoing, pastel-more shy

SILVER artistic color, creative, balanced

PERIWINKLE combination of indigo and violet attributes, quiet inner strength

You can send your message just by wearing the color.

Wear a Symbol Today

Next, let's address texture. Smooth texture is formal; heavy texture is informal and the most approachable. It used to be that people who didn't have as much money wore rough textures. It has evolved that casual clothes have rougher texture than dress-up clothes. Evening clothes are usually shiny and tightly woven. Corduroys and tweeds have the most texture and are more casual.

Line has messages. Vertical, straight lines give more authority and command attention. Think about pin-stripes. They are usually worn by people in high authority positions, at least traditionally—like bankers and lawyers. Curved lines are more approachable, less formal. Circular lines are playful (think of big rubber balls, the warm sun), and meandering lines are less dynamic. They aren't going anywhere in particular. That may not be a message you want to convey in your business life.

Pattern creates formal or informal tones. Jacquards are more professional than multicolored patterns. A controlled, uniform pattern is more professional than an abstract one. Small patterns are nonactive, almost nondescript, and often become simply a color while large patterns are lively, energetic, and attention-grabbing. Do clowns wear pinstripes in navy smooth wool gabardine? No, they will wear bright colors and bold prints when they entertain their audiences. Think about the messages you're sending with your choices.

Details finish an outfit and they have messages also. People are looking for certain symbols to assure them of your professionalism. How many people wear Rolex watches (or the equivalent) because of their strong message of success?

Details for a woman that demonstrate professionalism would include an outfit with a jacket, hose, dress shoes, and accessories (earrings, belt, watch, often a pin, scarf or necklace at neck). More casual symbols include mix-and-match pieces. Instead of wearing a suit where the pants and jacket are the same color, mix a taupe pant with a black jacket. Other elements of casual style are: texture, patterns and prints, and multiple colors rather than only one or two colors in an outfit. Accessories with movement or sound are more casual too.

The last thing people will notice in gathering evidence about you is your fit. Ill-fitting clothes send a sloppy message and lower your perceived IQ. Those things you don't think about because you're used to them may be the first things your audience spots — ill-fitting underwear or no underwear, slips that show, lining that's coming apart from a jacket. Be rigorous when dressing at home so you can get to the office and forget about your clothes.

Are Your Leggings Going to Work Today?

Here's the thing. Professional symbols can be mixed with casual symbols to make the right statement for your work situation or for your clients. A vet will have a different message to deliver than a lawyer. An advertising executive looks different than a judge. Law and finance share similar dress codes. Advertising and the fashion industry are more fashion-forward in their dress. By knowing the symbols of clothing, you can devise your own plan for what works at your work.

I've made an easy reference chart for you that demonstrates symbols of professional dress and casual dress. Now I know that lots of businesses are going casual, but think of this change as business attire that has been modified. The emphasis is still on business where you need to use professional symbols.

Professional/Formal

- **Color** navy, gray, dark shades, high contrast, one or two colors
- **Texture** smooth fabrics, fine and tight weaves

- **Pattern** small or faint pattern, solid lines, not broken, no pattern
- **Line** vertical, straight
- **Watch** metal band, fine leather
- **Jewelry** metal, no movement
- **Handbags** structured leather
- **Shoes** pumps

Casual / Informal

- **Color** light, bright, multiple colors, low to medium contrast
- **Texture** nubby tweeds, loose weaves, mix and match
- **Pattern** floral prints, abstracts, big, wild
- **Line** curved, circular, meandering
- **Watch** sports or novelty watch
- **Jewelry** dangly earrings, charm bracelets, bangles
- **Handbags** soft leathers, fabric
- **Shoes** open-toed sandals, tennis shoes

If you wear suits to work and your workplace is pretty formal, then the professional symbols are pretty straightforward. Run down the whole left side of this chart. You'd wear a navy blue, charcoal, or black suit, maybe in a faint pin-stripe. It's made out of wool gabardine, a tightly woven fabric. You'd wear button earrings (not dangly ones) and a pin on your lapel. You'd carry a leather handbag that is smooth and tidy and has a structured shape, maybe a rectangle. You'd wear hose and pumps. A no-brainer. Easy to figure out, easy to be appropriate when you follow the recipe. Everyone would look at you and know that you meant business.

If you showed up at that same workplace dressed in an orange and yellow Hawaiian print shirt and a loosely woven linen wrapskirt with Carmen Miranda dangly fruit earrings and open-toed sandals, your coworkers would not have a whole lot of confidence in your performance, nor would your clients. Your casual dress spells v-a-c-a-t-i-o-n from work, that's for sure.

Are you starting to see why there's been so much confusion with business casual? People went to their closets looking for casual clothes and put on those Hawaiian shirts and worn jeans, or worse, leggings. Yikes!

Let's take some symbols of professionalism and put them into a casual work setting. How about this? Wear a black casual pant (cotton lycra) with a white crisp cotton blouse and a cardigan sweater tied over the shoulders. Wear a smooth black belt and black loafers and a stainless steel watch. The high contrast of the black and white still gives a message of authority. The smooth fabrics are more professional, even though the pieces may be casual looking in themselves. The jewelry is more understated (professional) and the cardigan sweater is nonthreatening, a softer piece to wear than a blazer, making it more friendly, but more professional than two-piece dressing, which is dressing in a top and a bottom. That third piece—whether it's a sweater, cardigan, a softly structured jacket or a blazer—is a strong professional symbol.

Ready to tackle something a little more vague? How about "Business Party." The key word again here is business. And in business, you show no cleavage. You don't wear short skirts or dresses that hug the body tightly. This is a business function, not the place for you to let loose, hang loose, or hang out of your clothes. Use your business symbols and lean toward understatement. Wear a dress that glides over the body in a nonclingy fabric in a dark color. Think about it having some structure in the shoulder, or wear a coat-dress that has lapels. Structure and lapels are both professional symbols.

Are you having fun yet? This makes it easy to figure out, doesn't it? Once you know how to demonstrate professionalism, it's easy get dressed and feel confident that you are matching your clients' expectations of you and putting them immediately at ease. If you're working in a more casual setting, don't move far from the principles of professional dress.

Look sharp equals
be sharp.
That's the formula.
Now **get dressed** and **get to work.**

Going Places

*Has your social wardrobe got you
going nowhere? I don't want you to miss
out on any fun in your life,
so heavens–to–betsy, let's not have clothes
be the problem.*

LET ME INTRODUCE YOU TO A COUPLE OF PALS. Rita would be happy if her whole life could be handled in a suit. Suits, suits, suits. It's what she loves to buy, it's what she stocks her closet with, and when she gets the invitation to come to a "casual" surprise thirty-third birthday party on the thirtieth at three o'clock at the beach, she freaks. She's as comfortable in casual clothes as Shaquille O'Neal is in a pink tutu. I'm assuming.

Ellie is "Miss Casual." Jeans, cords, ribbed cotton T-shirts, lace-up all weather boots are her daily favorites. Although Montana lives in her heart, her address is Sausalito. The phone rings and her husband says, "Honey, you better have something for black tie. The boss has sponsored a table at this big fund-raiser. It's a 'have to' and it's on Saturday night." "Help!" she calls.

Everyone has her comfort zone, her freak-out zone, and right in the middle is the groan zone. "Do I have to go?" Yes, you said you'd go, you're going. Knowing what to wear gets you halfway there.

I'd like to give you some options other than freaking out and diving under the blankets to avoid an RSVP. Hopefully, shopping at the last minute won't be one of those options. When it's not in your closet and you have to buy something new to go to an event, there's even more pressure and more chance for error. What if you can't find it in time? Shopping last minute is as successful as grocery shopping when you're starving. You get home with four bags of groceries, but nothing to eat for dinner.

That, of course, is assuming that you even understand what is expected of your attire when you go somewhere. Remember when it was understood how you dressed to go to the opera? Now some folks go there in jeans. I don't recommend that.

Then there are gatherings at peoples' houses that can be confusing too. Lee got an invitation to a party and it said, "Casual Dress." Casual to her were shorts and a T-shirt, but when she got to the party everyone else was in skirts or dresses. She was mortified.

Has your social wardrobe got you going nowhere? I don't want you to miss out on any fun in your life, so heavens-to-betsy, let's not have clothes be the problem. Let me help you get you to your fund-raisers, weddings, house parties, the movies, theatre, dinners, lectures, and award ceremonies. With a simple formula, some examples, and a list of key pieces, you'll get there and maybe even have a great time. At least you won't be worrying about your clothes.

Let's start with "special." That's the basic formula right there. When you're going out, you need to look like you planned for this event. You don't want to make your host or your date think you gave no thought to this at all. That's disrespectful and it hurts you more than it hurts others, because you are mad at yourself all night and that's not fun.

Whether you are going to a party, the ballet, or a fund-raiser, you need to have at least one stand-out special piece on. It could be a leopard print mule, a sequined top, a darling little handbag, or elegant textured hosiery. (Check out the Dressy Capsule in the Capsules Anyone? chapter for a quick social fix for any outfit.)

Having a couple of simple clothing pieces in black or metallic dressy colors that can be worn together for the dressiest of occasions and separated and worn in a ratio of one to one, one dressy piece with one nondressy piece for more casual social events can get you just about anywhere. A dressy pant and tunic with the Dressy Capsule accessories (from **Capsules Anyone?**) will go to many fancy affairs. Take that dressy tunic (in silk satin for instance) and put it over a wool crepe pant with pumps and it's ready to go to a nice restaurant for dinner or a casual chic house party.

You've heard the concept of day-and-night dressing where what you wear to the office for day can be the core of what you wear out to dinner that night by just slipping into the rest room at work and doing a couple of magic tricks and you're instantly transformed. I love those tricks and I want to share some with you. Even if you aren't working, look at the possibilities for outfits to your next social engagement.

What you're changing from office to social is mood. So we want to take the seriousness or professionalism out of our outfits and slip into a mood-altering ensemble. Usually the ingredients for that are sparkle, shine, skin, something sexy (sometimes), and clothes that are special somehow. A social wardrobe needs specialty items. A shiny blouse, interesting texture in a jacket, necklines that bare a lot of skin, skirts that slit, pants that flow, unsensible shoes (could be comfortable and still be unsensibly sexy) that show more foot—these are the tools of a quick-change artist.

Here are some things that you can be on the lookout for:

Interesting tops. A simple blouse, worn outside of a pant in a shimmery fabric with little detail in a fantastic color—either bright and exciting (orange, kiwi green, watermelon red) or elegant, regal, and refined (platinum, cream, taupe) can transform an ordinary day outfit into an evening ensemble with great pizzaz or flair.

A sequined or beaded stretchy T-shirt. These are good to look for on sale when you're cruising a department store. They seem to be easier to find when you're not looking for normal clothes. They'll pop out at you on the sale rack. This simple shaped garment could transform a business suit and say, "Let's party!"

A printed blouse. Blouses in a bright, splashy design say "Fun," especially if they are in a fluid fabric or have a shimmery, smooth texture.

A decorative sweater. I think you'll know one when you see one, but it could have a beaded border or crystal buttons or sequins scattered on it to distinguish it from a work sweater.

A beautiful shawl in a dressy fabric (taffeta or a sheer chiffon with appliqué, or a rich-colored velvet shawl) will go over a black suit that you sneak out of your business wardrobe lineup and transform into evening wear with just that little cover-up action.

Evening bag or novelty party bag. An evening bag is a lot smaller than your work bag. Think of it as the size of an envelope, not an 8½-by-11 inch, but one you would use for a business or personal letter or a greeting card. We're talking small. Look for ones that are in dressy fabrics or for fun, casual parties, something colorful will be great.

Mules or strappy sandals. Try on dozens of pairs of strappy sandals until you find a pair that you can walk a few blocks in.

If you can't walk around the shoe department **without pain,** nestle them back in the tissue paper and box that they came in and **keep looking**.

A business suit, which you were wearing at 5 o'clock with your pumps, becomes a sexy suit when you change the shoes to something more open, slip into that sexy sequined or beaded T-shirt, and then add a shawl for a wrap. Voila! Instant socializing. Don't wear nylons with open-toed sandals. Wear slingbacks if you want to wear nylons.

A color burst. In a blouse, a bag, a shoe, a pant. One special somewhere, put color.

Remember Miss Casual whom you met earlier? She likes comfort, and I'd put her in a pull on velvet or silk pant with an elastic waistband. I'd add a tunic—either matching or in another texture, but the same color. Add a long necklace with some drama, a dressy pump, and a small dressy handbag. Keep it all in the same tone—all black, all taupe, all charcoal. This is a soft silhouette, easy, comfortable, doable, and it won't freak out a casual freak like Ellie.

For suit-lover Rita, going to the party at the beach is definitely not in her comfort zone. I'd put her in separates like a cotton/Lycra blend pant, a scoopneck T-shirt, and a linen, slightly structured, short jacket with three-quarter sleeves and a collar. She'll feel closer to the elements of the suit she's used to in this outfit than if we put her in a flowing summer dress and espadrilles.

There is always a way to go to something that's out of your comfort range. Think about what the dress code is anticipated to be and then find a meeting place between what you're comfortable in and what is appropriate. If this is a tough wardrobe area for you, do your best to determine what the dress code will be where you are going. When you get to the event, get your glass of wine, relax—and then observe. What are others wearing? If it was billed as a casual party, see how others interpreted that. Was it a nice pair of slacks and a sweater set with pretty jewelry? Was it a casual printed dress? Was it blue jeans and an interesting top? Collect data for future reference. There's going to be a wide variety. Find a way to stay true to yourself and your comfort while honoring the occasion.

Wearing blue jeans to everything is a cop-out. The question is how can you create a bridge so you can be comfortable with yourself while being comfortable in the setting you're going into? You have many ways to do it—with color, pattern, texture, fabrics, shapes. When you're working in unfamiliar turf, remember, you don't have to go all the way—just borrow one or two things from the formal or informal spectrum that we talked about in the last chapter—so that you're joining in the right mood for the event.

If you are confused about what to wear, let color be your guiding friend. Look at the color chart in the Going to Work chapter and relate color to your social commitment. Are you going to a party where you're feeling really outgoing and ready for a lot of interaction? Wear yellow. Do you want to convey a sensitivity and an allure of exoticness? Try violet. Feeling romantic? Wear pink. Want to keep them guessing? **Wear black.**

Okay, you're more ready to go than when we first started. However, if it's a costume party you're going to, I have a confession to make. The only place I'm nervous about letting you down is in this area of costume parties. If you're following my advice and getting your closet nice and Zen, you don't have any 70s or 80s dusty relics freeloading in there. Costume parties are the big groan for me, but I realize they are pure delight for fellow earth travelers. If you are one of those, then hang on to those real doozies that would make great costumes and stash them in a spare closet or a box that fits under your bed. Have fun being an 80s chick.

Everything You Must Know about Underwear

The outsides of your clothes are only as good as the foundations they rest on— your underwear. Try building a house on a sagging foundation. Big trouble.

SCARLET O'HARA KNEW A LOT ABOUT UNDERWEAR. She knew that what happened under the dress made a huge difference with how the dress looked to her admirers—or maybe it was her maidservant, Mammy, who understood it best. Remember in the movie *Gone with the Wind* how Scarlet would hold onto the bedpost while Mammy would tighten up her corset? Makes you wonder how she did all that jabbering with Ashley and Rhett when she was tightened up so much she could hardly breath. Oh, but she looked good in those dresses!

There have been a lot of movements since Scarlet O'Hara was romping around Tara in whalebone corsets. There was that bra-burning thing in the 60s—although I heard there really weren't that many bras burned, but it was a great symbol for the fight for equality. We've come a long way, Baby, but in some ways, we never got too far away from Scarlet and Tara. Women still want to look good in their clothes and hey, there's nothing like good underwear to do the trick. The outsides of your clothes are only as good as the foundations they rest on—your underwear. Try building a house on a sagging foundation. Big trouble. Get those tool belts on, Girls, we're going to work on foundations.

Remember your first bra? Maybe your mother took you to a department store and let Heloise measure you to get the right size. Oh my god, I was so embarrassed! Heloise came up with 32 A in one style. That's all I could handle in the dressing room. I wanted out of there. I remember getting home and taking them out of their special boxes in the privacy of my bedroom. I held them up. They were pristine bras in a white that was brighter than snow.

Fast-forward a bunch of years to shopping for bras with my teenage daughter Erin who only lives life in matching bra and undie sets, lots of bra and undie sets. She tricked me into shopping with her one day after church, and we walked down to the Macy's in San Francisco for an afternoon of trying on pretty bras and underwear. The lingerie department at Macy's is like going to Costco. There must be 22,000 square feet of metal fixtures jammed with little clear plastic hangers holding bras and undies that either break or fall off by the handfuls the minute you touch one.

We spent three hours there; I'm not kidding. While my daughter was gathering twelve sets of bras and undies at a time, I paced the department, fidgeting until I decided to get Zen about this, give in, and try some bras on myself. I slipped off my blouse and tried on black ones, peach ones, white ones, cream ones, polka-dotted ones. And then something really weird happened. I tried on a navy-blue one. God, it was gorgeous. Lace from it-had-to-be France. I swear, I looked in the mirror and saw something I hadn't seen since my 32B days, I was looking UP. I felt like I was on top of the Empire State Building or something. Uplifted. Ready to belt out the "Star Spangled Banner." I was reaching for the stars, facing heaven—in my navy-blue full-figured Wacoal bra. I had just had a conversion, like on the road to Damascus.

I wasn't sure if I was seeing correctly. I called in Delores who was working that end of the floor. "Is this the right size for me?" I asked. She stood behind me in the dressing room and peered over my shoulder at the reflection in the mirror. "Just a minute," she said and grabbed the adjusters on the straps and in one quick movement she yanked them up and let them go. The slapping sound against my back startled me almost as much as looking at myself with breasts way *up there*. She hoisted those babies up like a crane on California Street lifting a beam up to the tenth floor of the office buildings under construction one block away. "There," she said, satisfied. "Now that's a good fit."

A good fit. I don't think I've had a good fit for twenty years! Oh, man, was I excited! Whoooeeee! I tried five more styles. My daughter asked what I thought of this one or that one from the dressing room next door. I couldn't have cared a hoot. I was busy finding matching panties.

Underwear Overhaul

Bras are the number one thing that women wear that are the wrong size. Well, undies too. You keep buying the same size you were in high school, regardless of how your body has changed.

Bras aren't like polio vaccines. You don't just get one once. You go back and do it again and again, and you get refitted again and again so you're always in the right size.

Here's what to expect. The way one is measured for bras is by using a cloth tape measure and measuring in three places. If you're doing this yourself, slip the tape measure under the arm, but above the breast where a sleeveless gown would come across. Write that number down. This is your body size.

Second, put your arms down, take a breath and measure around the apex, at the fullest part of the breast. Write that number down.

Third, measure the rib cage, directly underneath the breast. Have your bra on or if it's ill-fitting, you can unhook the bra and have a little lift while you do the measurement. If the rib cage measurement is even, add four to the number, if it's odd, add five. The total number is your band size.

If the second measurement is one inch more than your body size, your bra cup size is an A. If it's two inches more than your body size, your cup size is a B. Three inches bigger and you are a C-cup. Four inches more and you are a D-cup.

The underarm measurement is used mainly as confirmation of the rib cage. If this is puzzling in the least, do yourself a magnificent favor and put yourself in the hands of an expert. There are plenty of them around, and believe me, breasts vary like crazy. There are shallow breasts, full ones, firm ones, saggy ones, one breast is a different size than the other (you're normal!), lots of variables. There are other variables too. Fabric stretch in bras can put you in a size that's different than your measuring size would indicate. These measurements are *guides*. Your job is to hang in there and get the undergarments that FIT. If something isn't fitting you, it's the fault of the manufacturer, not you. Keep trying things on.

Here's a little test I want you all to do. Stand in front of a full-length mirror. Look at your shoulders and draw an imaginary line across them. Put your hands at your waist and draw an imaginary line across your waist. Now look at your bustline. Is it in the middle, heading north or heading south? If it's in the middle or higher, you're doing great, maybe even looking perky. If it's lower than the middle, you will be looking older and heavier than you actually are—not the look we're going for. Often this can be remedied by just adjusting the bra straps and lifting those babies higher. If this doesn't do the trick, a push-up bra could lift that line up for you.

Try to get away from any connotations you might have with terms. Don't ever make your breasts wrong! Don't say bad things about them! Get educated instead. For instance, "full-figured" doesn't mean "fat lady." A full-figured bra is a more generous cut. It's what you need to eliminate double vision—that double boob thing where you see breast tissue falling out of the bra through a woman's knit top. It jiggles. No jiggling, Ladies. Jiggling equals bad fit. The double boob comes from a full bust trying to fit into a demi-cup (which is an appropriate style for an A or a B cup woman). It's like trying to get a cup and a half of sugar into a one cup measuring device. No can do.

A tell-tale sign of a bra that will give you full-figured gals the support you need is that the shoulder straps will be wider. These are better for you, my dear, because they relieve back and shoulder discomfort. And the hooks in the back come in rows of threes or fours. No single or even double hooks for you.

When you are buying bras, you want to start out wearing your bra on the middle hook. When it needs washing, you are fastening it tighter. When it's washed, go back to the middle hook. If you wear it on the loosest hook, the fabric can rub against your skin.

Padding is available in all cup sizes and is good for full-figured women particularly when you are wearing T-shirts or knits. You want to have a bra that is smooth. You don't want any visions of lace leakage, where you can see the lace pattern on the outside of your clothes. The smooth padding (this is not a padded bra, just a smooth cup with a teeny bit of lining) cuts down on nipple explosion as well.

If it's a padded bra you are wanting, a new product on the market is the water bra. Padded cups are filled with water so it really feels natural. No kidding. Also, you can add waterlike inserts that slip into the bottom of the bra which forces your own breast tissue up, giving women cleavage who never thought they'd see it staring back at them in a full-length mirror. It's a wonderful thing. The other thing that a padded bra does is create more fullness in your upper torso that can visually balance more fullness in the hips. Just another reason to consider this as an option.

Don't Double Your Fun

Here's another opportunity to correct double vision. You've seen this—the double butt line—where there is a double line formed by the natural curve of your buttocks and then the artificial line of a panty that's riding up another four inches either because of the style of it or because it's too small. Regardless of the reason, it is a look I'd like you all to get rid of. Undies are another place where a woman may be wearing the same style she wore when she was twelve, that may not be the right choice for her in the body that she is currently in.

Regardless of your favorite style of undies, I need to say something here about gramma undies, the full brief. Okay, gramma undies is not a technical or fair term, but I say it because you think it and I want you to get that image out of your minds. Cool chicks wear full briefs. A lot of lines can be eliminated by going all the way to the waist with your underwear. There's that dip over the bikini line in front of bikini underwear that comes from non-abs-of-steel. Those lines formed by panties make the bulges look bigger than they actually are. What works in other clothing works in underwear too — buy a size larger to look a size smaller. When you are trying on underwear in a dressing room, it's a little awkward, but put them on over your own and see if the style is right for you! You should fall in love with the fit of your underwear, the color, the fabric, the style — but always start with fit first. That means you need to try those babies on.

Thongs. "They're really comfortable!" a Las Vegas dancer told me once. I believed her. I got so fed up once with a pair of thong underwear that a salesperson convinced me was "really comfortable," that I did what I'd never expected myself to do. I was in a meeting, excused myself, went to the bathroom, took them off, tossed them in the same trash as the hand towels, and then went back to the meeting. I was wearing pants.

My cutie-pie daughters have said for years, "Mom, they're so comfortable!" One of them bought me one for a present. It got stuffed way back in my underwear drawer, but when I was going to be on TV wearing my slim close-fitting pants, I knew I didn't want a panty line so I pulled them out. You know what? They weren't bad! Here's the key—what my daughter was trying to tell me all along—which is that you want that butt floss part to be really thin, really soft. It helps to find a thong where the fabric is real stretchy and in an open, loose weave. Even in thongs, *particularly* in thongs, you have to go for comfort over cute. Less is better. Wide will feel like a wedgie. Frilly stuff gets in the way. Be sure you buy the thong large enough so that you don't get any fat over the sides of the hip/waist area where the thin band comes up. You don't want it so tight that it looks like you've tied a string tight around your hips.

If you're not going to try the thong and you absolutely do not want a panty line, here's your solution: panty hose with built-in underwear that includes a cotton-lined crotch. Add a panty liner pad to absorb moisture during the day. These panty hose come in a capri length so your feet are free and you can wear sandals even with your pants. Or as one client does, just cut normal panty hose off so they stop just below the knee for that smooth butt and thigh look in pants.

Lingerie Tech

Body shapers are another tool to be found in the lingerie department. Body shapers are available for any jiggling body part. You can get ones that slim tummies, or butts, or thighs, or the whole thing—in slips that hug it all in so you can wear a slinky dress and be smooth. You wouldn't want to wear many of these body shapers for eight hours. A four-hour stint (say the length of a party) is probably all you want to do before you're longing for your flannel bathrobe with nothing underneath it. And I'd also suggest that there not be a lot of eating going on while you're wearing these. Digestion can be hampered by these devices or at least it can feel that way.

There are such great tools in a lingerie department. Really, you should go and browse like you would browse a bookstore. Pick things up, take a look, read about them, ask questions from the experts in the department, and go try some things on. There are things there that you didn't even know existed. Technology creates more and more options all the time for achieving comfort and shape in undergarments. The menu of available styles and solutions is mind-blowing. And then there's another opportunity to express your style in your underwear. Maybe you are the cotton undies sporty kind of gal, or the French undies vavavoom kind of gal who goes for the lace all the way, or maybe you're somewhere in-between or a little bit of both. There are about a thousand styles in-between those two. Come on, express yourself! Take a mini-vacation in the lingerie department and come out of it refreshed and happy in undies that are perfect for you. Like the hair color commercial says, "You're worth it."

Now repeat after me: "I will be fitted every year or so (especially if I have a weight gain or loss) for new bras. I will forget about size and go for fit especially in my underwear. I will wear comfortable underwear that fits me right so my clothes look great and I feel good all day." The quality of your life while being in good-fitting underwear versus being in bad-fitting underwear is like driving through Friday traffic as a passenger in a fully-equipped shimmering new limousine versus being the driver of a sputtering mud-caked, banged up itty bitty tinny car in need of an overhaul with a gas gauge on empty.

You deserve the best. **Go get it.**

Yikes! Bikes! and Other Sport Gear

Leave the one hundred
percent Lycra all-the-time
to the people who have earned it
—the class instructors and
the personal trainers.
It's a respect thing, an honor thing.
You don't get to wear
priest robes just because
you like the look.

TODAY WE'RE GOING SHOPPING FOR EXERCISE CLOTHES.
"Exercise clothes, Bren?" You betcha! This is another place
where you wear clothes. Why shouldn't your exercise wardrobe
be as delightful, purposeful, and exquisite—in it's own way—as
the rest of your wardrobe? Why feel great in all other areas of life
and then schlumpy in this one? No, that's not our plan for your
healthy wardrobe self. It is bliss finding the workout pant that
you can't wait to put on and exercise in. You think of your
favorite workout T-shirt and you've burned fifty calories just getting excited about slipping it over your head.

The other reason I want to talk about exercise clothes (EC) is that unused and unloved EC can take up a lot of space on shelves, in drawers, on closet floors. I want some air and light and aliveness in this part of your wardrobe — and some breathing room where it is stored.

Let me tell you what happens with exercise clothes. I could be telling your story right here! Let's talk about running T-shirts and if this isn't your sport, substitute a piece of clothing from whatever yours is. When I'm in the closet with you and I see eighty-eight running/exercise/camping T-shirts, I'm going to say, "Do you realize you have eighty-eight T-shirts here?" And before you answer, I can tell you how they all got there. First of all, there are the ones you earned from races you ran in. They have sentimental value attached to them, even if they aren't in your top fifteen current favorites that you grab for.

Then there are the T-shirts that you used to wear as day clothes that got a stain on it that you couldn't get out. So you turned it into a running T-shirt. There's the T-shirt you wore one day while you were flying and the ink pen you were writing with started leaking from the pressurized cabin and you got a big ink mark all over it. It turned into a running T-shirt. Pretty soon you have downshifted clothes from one part of your life to this part of your life *and*, although this made sense at the time, do you really need eighty-eight T-shirts? Do you wear all of those eighty-eight T-shirts? No. Let me hear it from your own lips: "No, Bren, I really don't need eighty-eight running T-shirts."

Okay, here's what we're going to do. We're going to get honest and go through that pile of T-shirts and clear a good many of them out. You don't need to be using precious shelf space to store things you aren't wearing.

First off, I'm not going to make you get rid of those sentimental favorites. I'm not that mean. But, I am going to ask you to pull those from the stack and store them in a Sentimental Favorites box/bag/vault. Do this with warm-up pants, with bike clothes, with hiking clothes. Pull out the souvenir clothes and put them in a loved place away from your closet. Then skim off your very favorites, the ones you can't wait to wear tomorrow. Now separate out the ones that are just plain shot, the ones you're ready to turn into rags or send to their resting point in a nearby landfill. Be honest. Do it. EC come in and out of style and they should **COME IN AND GO OUT OF YOUR CLOSET** when they have expired physically or emotionally.

What's left? A section of ambivalence. Things you kinda like. We have a family technical term created by my daughter Erin when she was really young; it's a good one to pull out and use at this time. When asked what she thought of a certain food, she said, "I kinda like it, but I mostly hate it." Try that on for size with this last section. Do you kinda like them but mostly hate them? Be honest. You may whittle a few more off the pile using this measuring stick. I want your exercise clothes to be a joy to put on, so move out the dumpy, schlumpy ones now.

Here's the thing. For some of us, exercise is tough enough to fit into our lives, so if we can generate conditions that will draw us in or keep us engaged, let's do it. Let's choose EC in the colors we love, the fabrics we prefer, the styles that are the most flattering. There are flattering yoga pants and then there are *unflattering* ones.

Cotton is Rotten

Okay, are you psyched to get into the dressing room now? I have to admit that another reason I'm so crazy about EC shopping is that all the really cool fabric technology gets its start in this department of the store. Scientists and designers are concocting ways to make your exercise clothes keep you dryer, cooler, and more comfortable while doing your ab work or your flexes or your sprints. It's not just about looking cool; it's about helping your body out during these intense workouts.

For instance, wearing beloved cotton, although it breathes, is the worst. It holds water when you sweat and if you are sweating in temperatures cooler than your body temperature, it cools down while evaporating and you can get hypothermia quite easily. The best thing is to get water away from the skin. This is possible with the new fabrics that wick the moisture away from you. The more comfortable you are (and healthy) while doing your sport, the more you'll keep at it. You advance in the sport quicker when you do the little things that make the big difference, starting with dressing to be comfortable.

Fashion and function are enjoying a great marriage in the bike world. Men's dominance in the sport is being challenged by the growing numbers of women flocking to biking as well as the sport of spinning (working out on special stationary bikes in classes led by a gym instructor). This has spurred manufacturers to create complete lines of bike sport clothes cut with women's bodies in mind.

For instance, men and women are not created equally, and bike shorts take into consideration the difference in their body parts, especially where the butt hits the bike seat. Padded bike shorts make riding long distances much more comfortable, and although styles may be similar to both genders, the pads aren't, so pick one from the women's section.

You could wear a ragged, holey '93 Monterey Jazz Festival T-shirt to ride in, but here's what you get when you wear a jersey instead. Jerseys in technical fabrics (that wick moisture away) or in one hundred percent wool, famous for being warm in the winter and cool in the summer, come with long zippers in front, so if you've worked up a big sweat, unzip the front a ways for some instant cool down. Jerseys are cut longer in the back so when you're bent over your handlebars, your shirt won't ride up. Jerseys come with back zipper pouches, triple pockets, or single pockets that can hold a rolled-up windbreaker, maps, arm warmers, or cash for lattes down at my local coffee shop (or yours) when you come down off the hills.

Besides advanced fabrics, there is more variety in styles. If skintight isn't your thing, there's baggy. Some garments actually look like casual street clothes, but they have built in pads for comfort in the bottom. A woman can pick out a skirt that looks like a skirt from the front and shorts from the back but has padding inside. Or she can stick to Lycra in the basic shorts, knee-length knickers, or capri-length pants for more coverage.

The Half & Half Plan

I don't know about you, but seeing bodies in skintight Lycra from head to calves scares me. It's more information than I need about people I don't know. For this reason, I think that a half and half plan, half-baggy and half-skintight, is a good one. A baggy padded riding short would team nicely with a sleeveless jersey.

Let's take that half and half plan into running, training, or classes at the YMCA. Leave the one hundred percent Lycra all-the-time to the people who have earned it—the class instructors and the personal trainers. It's a respect thing, an honor thing. You don't get to wear priest robes just because you like the look. You earn them. And those instructors in one hundred percent Lycra have put the required hours into their profession in order to earn the right to wear all Lycra, all the time. Except for the grocery store. Even they have to give Lycra a rest.

Here's the wardrobe plan while you're earning your stripes. Pick a top or a bottom. Lather in Lycra on your top half or your bottom half, your choice. You could:

1. wear a sport tank top—a sports bra within a tank top—with soccer shorts or baggy athletic bottoms, or
2. a looser T-shirt with spandex shorts or tighter warm-up pants.

If you wear spandex shorts or pants, watch for the double butt action. Wear a thong or no underwear so you don't get that double butt line from underwear riding up.

Can you mix and match "labels"? Oh yes. Adidas, Fila, Nike, New Balance, or Reebok would love to have your full loyalty, but it isn't necessary. Ready-to-wear designers, like DKNY, are big in the exercise-wear market as well. The key is to get into the dressing room and try things on.

Don't be suspicious of retailers. They are stocking shelves with products that will entice you to get out there and make the most of your exercise time while supplying you with the latest technology to help you feel good and look good while you're doing it.

Caring for
Those Babies

If you're going to wear clothes,
you can count on this:
> *Stuff Happens*

EVERY TIME WE'RE IN THE DRESSING ROOM TOGETHER and
you've got on this dynamite outfit that you can't wait to buy, I
imagine it living permanently like it is today. Perfect. When I
look into the future, I never see a knit sagging, or a lining coming
undone, or an ink pen leaving a mark on that champagne-colored
leather jacket.

I have undying faith in your new clothes and mine as well. I
never imagine that something could change the landscape of my
currently favorite long silk wrapskirt, so when I'm at my friend
Tim's house for Thanksgiving and his pet rabbits pedal over to
where I'm sitting ("They are soooooo c-u-t-e!!!!"), I am stunned
when in three precious seconds fluffy Rose Prozac has eaten a
two-inch square area of my precious skirt!

If you're going to wear clothes, you can count on this: Stuff
Happens. You can buy backups. Some people do. If a rabbit eats
their skirt, there's another one at home that's never been worn. But
as soon as they put the backup on, they are back out there living
on the edge of life where a cat in the lap could mean pulled threads,
or drinking coffee in the car with a loose lid could mean coffee lap.

It's a wild world out there. Let me give you some tools to handle it, starting with the Serenity Prayer: *God grant me the serenity to accept the things I cannot change* ("I didn't know the lid was loose! Now I'll have to take this dress to the cleaners because it's not washable. Darn."), *the courage to change the things I can* ("If I don't want to be at the cleaners all the time, I'll check the labels more closely in the things I buy and go for washable things."), *and the wisdom to know the difference* (Read the labels! Machine washing Dry Clean Only items can lead to disastrous results).

Clean Up Your Act

Why don't we just start right there at the cleaners? Here's a fact, well, if not a fact, at least a strong opinion—mine! Your clothes will live longer the fewer times they visit the dry cleaners, so do a few things to curtail their visits:

1. Hang your Dry Clean Only jackets or pants outside in the fresh air to freshen them up between wearings. Another quick refresher: hang them in the bathroom while your shower is running to steam the wrinkles out.

2. Hang your clothes up after wearing. Some people take a look at their clothes after leaving them on the floor and because they're looking messy they throw them in the bag headed for the cleaners. Unnecessary!

3. Get friendly with spot removers and follow their directions. Energine is a friend to many. Also handy is a toothbrush. You can avoid a lot of dry cleaning bills with this little trick. That toothbrush (not the one you are currently using) can take surface stains out. Sweet potatoes, mashed potatoes—that kind of thing—will loosen up and come off the sleeve edges of jackets and shirts. Just rub across them with the toothbrush once they are dry.

Okay, so what do you do when the packet of dressing you were squeezing hard because you didn't tear enough of an opening across the top of it lets loose and deposits its contents all over you—and your Dry Clean Only shirt and pant—instead of the lettuce greens? Well, it's time for a visit to the cleaners. Did you know that you have a choice of cleaning processes? Cleaners aren't all created equally. Although most cleaners use the potent (and toxic) chemical "perchloroethylene" (perc) to clean your clothes, there are cleaners that use drylene instead (very popular in Europe), a nontoxic, environmentally safe chemical that is gentler on your fine fabrics, highly effective, and doesn't have that awful smell that we often associate with dry cleaning. You might want to check it out. If your clothes are cleaned with perc, air them out in the garage for a few days, outside of the plastic bag before you store them.

Bad things happen to clothes that are stored away for months with soiled spots on them. While you're shifting summer clothes out of your closet and making room for your winter ones, do the right thing. Take those summer Dry Clean Only silks, linens, and tropical weight wools to the cleaners and have them cleaned before you store them. Fruit juice stains, for instance, get worse over time and often are impossible to get out months later.

Here are some things that can save you grief and money at the cleaners:

1. Take Responsibility from the Start. It's imperative to the life of your garment to read the care instructions. There are hundreds of new fabrics that show up on the market each month. Manufacturers have determined how to care for that garment and they've reported that to you by way of the label sewn in the sideseam or at the neck of the garment. *Read it and obey*. If you fall in love with an expensive garment that is different than your everyday fabric or has a fiber content that you're unfamiliar with, buy it from a company that has good customer service. You want to be able to go back to the store if there's a problem and say, "I expected a longer life than the couple of weeks I had it before I cleaned it and it got damaged." The manufacturer of the garment may be experimenting with blends or new techno fabrics and is making the best determination they can about its care. The fiber/fabric business is changing rapidly. New things are coming on the market constantly. Occasionally they're wrong about how to care for something. A good retailer will back you up and refund your money if it didn't perform the **way you expected it to.**

Linda in Atlanta told me her story, which is a vote for working with a good retailer who can afford to back up their merchandise. Linda shopped for a mother-of-the-bride dress, a pretty darn important dress. She found something at Saks Fifth Avenue, but the dress needed altering. Even though she went back more than once for fittings, they just weren't getting it to fit properly. They offered to give her money back. That was fine, but it put her in a time pinch with the wedding coming up. She went to Neiman Marcus and fell in love with a gorgeous designer gown that was only in the store for a day as part of a trunk show. The staff at Neiman's got on the phone with the designer to see if Linda could buy the sample in the store that day. The designer said okay and

Linda got the perfect gown. She hadn't planned to spend that kind of money on a dress, but it being such an important event, she closed her eyes and handed over her credit card. She wore it to the wedding, but after only one wearing, it was pilling badly. She took it back to Neiman's to show them before she got it cleaned at the dry cleaners and they said, "Don't bother, we'll give you your money back."

It wasn't her intention, but Linda ended up wearing a gorgeous gown for free. Of course, these things do endear us to the big retailers and keep us coming back. I recently took back a pant when it seemed to grow a whole size in one wearing. No questions asked, full refund.

2. 'Fess Up Immediately. Stains are treated differently, with different methods, and different chemicals, which only a professional will determine. Tell your professional the whole truth. Brown may be brown to you, but to a dry cleaner brown stains are not all the same. Tell your dry cleaner it's the spaghetti sauce or the bloodstain. He then uses the right chemical the first time. If you don't tell him, each time he tries to get a stain out there's a chance of pulling out color or wearing the garment out.

3. God is in the Details and the Details Go to the Dry Cleaners. You just love those denim jeans with the really groovy red suede detail along the bottom hem. You love them so much you rip the tags off and wear them for five days in a row. On the sixth day, you spill coffee all over them. You go to wash them and happen to read the care instructions and it says, "Dry Clean Only—with a leather specialist." Oh yes, you're sending those babies to the dry cleaners and it's going to cost you $25 because they're specialists. Should you have not bought those cutie-pie jeans that you love? Well, if you hate the cleaners and the bills that accrue there, yeah, put them back in their neat little pile at the store. If you're willing to take them to the specialists when they need to go, buy them and love them. They're worth it. Again, read those labels. If a denim or a cotton that normally goes into the washer and dryer has a special ribbon or fabric trim, it may very well need that special treatment. You won't be paying for that garment once. You'll pay and pay and pay if it lives at the cleaners. Just want you to think that through.

4. Sort Your Clothes as Mother Said. Have a laundry hamper that is designated for dry cleaning only. Make it a different color than your regular laundry hamper so you don't mix your dry cleaning items up with your regular wash. How many times have you accidentally thrown a Dry Clean Only item into your washer and, when you pulled it out, discovered that it had shrunk three sizes or that it was permanently wrinkled and there was nothing you could do about it? I'd done it plenty until I bought that blue laundry basket for me and my family's dry cleaning items. That special basket could live in the laundry room or the family member's room with the most laundry issues.

Remember the Serenity Prayer? About changing the things you can? There are some other things you can have the courage to do before you're stuck with a garment that doesn't perform the way you wished it had. While you're still in the dressing room with the tags on or at home in front of your full-length mirror with the tags still on, test-drive clothes. Sit, stretch, walk, turn, move around. See if you can determine how this garment is going to perform. See if seams strain and the fabric doesn't want to give. This could mean trouble in less than a week. One wearing could make the fibers pull apart from the seam and leave gaps along the stress points — along the bottom or across the shoulders.

Another thing to pay attention to is sound. When you walk or move your arms, does the fabric make a rustle that irritates you after five minutes? If you're wearing a jacket made from a fabric that is noisy, you could be nearly crazy by the time you walk to your bus stop. In the dressing room, I'm always aware of the noise of clothes. It's something you may not notice as you're falling in love with the color and the cut, but I've known a few garments that never got reached for in the closet because they were too loud.

How badly does it wrinkle? I don't want you to do the crunching-a-handful-of-fabric-inside-a-tight-fist test. That's not what you normally do with clothes. Just do the things you normally do. Sit, scrunch down, bend, sit some more, then stand up and take a sober look in the mirror.

Susan bought a dress for a party. She brought it to the party on a hanger, slipped into it while there and stood the whole time. It was great. She wore it two weeks later and sat in a car with a seat belt on all the way to a wedding. When she got out of the car and looked down, it looked as if she'd slept in the dress. If she'd test-driven the dress in the dressing room, she'd have discovered this. Everything looks so gorgeous and indestructible on a hanger, steamed and pristine. Your body is not a hanger. It has movable parts. See what happens to the clothes when you move in them.

The At-Home Disaster Quiz

Now I've got a few other bright ideas to pass along that fall into the category of "I-can't-believe-I-just-did-that" at-home disasters.

Take this little quiz to find the solutions:

1. You're at my house eating my famous homemade blueberry pancakes. You cut a piece with your fork and that fresh, steaming blueberry bursts open and splatters your top with blueberry guts. You scream, "Oh, my God!" and then you:

   a. blot it with soda water

   b. use a little dish soap, warm water, and a washcloth and go at it with your fingertips

   c. take your washable cotton or linen or blended blouse to my kitchen sink, turn on the hot water and stand there until it's really steaming and then slide the blueberry stain under the running water and hold it there while the water dissolves it completely away

   Now, if you're coming to my house for blueberry pancakes, I will have already told you to bring an extra shirt with you in case this happens, because it happens often, but if it's your only one and you're eating these pancakes or anything else that's berry-sourced at someone else's house or in a restaurant, it's your call as to whether you race home and treat this right away. Faster is better. And the answer is **c.** This really works, every time.

2. You're at my house and there's a party going on. Someone goes to kiss you and misses. The kiss—and a bright smudge of lipstick—lands on the collar of your favorite blouse. What do you do?

   a. scream

   b. take soap and water after it and scrub scrub scrub

   c. ask me for some hairspray, spray the lipstick, and then dab it away with a clean washcloth

   The answer is **c.** But test the hairspray first on a piece of the blouse that doesn't show. Do not rub and scrub. Dab. The hairspray lifts the stain up and out and the clean washcloth captures it. It's a miracle!

3. You're *almost* at home. You're at a spiritual outdoor retreat. You're sitting at an iron table and when you get up, you see the dry rust spot that mars your dress. What do you do?
   a. go to your room and cry
   b. try the hair spray trick
   c. dilute a bit of shampoo in water, rinse out the garment and hang to dry

The answer is **c**. Yes, *clear* shampoo comes to the rescue. Again, wet and test the fabric first to be sure it doesn't leave a water mark.

The *Emergency* Road Kit

The last thing I want to leave you with is the idea of having an Emergency Road Kit packed away in the trunk of your car. It will help you handle those things that can happen while you're out and about doing life. This is easy. Get a shoebox or the equivalent of one and pack it with those things that can be lifesavers when Something Happens. Here are some things that live in my Emergency Road Kit (ERK):

corn pads for a toe that bothers me in certain shoes or to soften the clip of a clip-on earring—I'll put one on the clip part that hugs the back of my ear

packing tape that I use to delint my clothes—works better than a lintbrush

an extra lipstick in case I lose mine

toothbrush to brush up suede shoes or a suede jacket that might get spotted, or for that sleeve edge in case I dangle it too close to the mashed potatoes I have for lunch. Remember, it's the first line of defense before heading to the dry cleaners.

extra pair of hose in case I get a run

a compact, shadows, and blush that are just about used up in case I'm out for a long day and need touch-ups (I don't carry makeup in my purse, just lipstick)

Band-Aids in case of blisters in new shoes

deodorant in case I forgot to put it on in the morning—yes, this does happen to me and I bet it's happened to you, too. Rather than worry about it, plan for the possibility and stash some in your ERK.

Good luck caring for your well-chosen, beautiful, beloved clothes. Watch out for rabbits. Speaking of which, do you want to know what happened to my skirt? I took it to the cleaners and had the alterations person there creatively cut a new line to the edge. Now the wraparound skirt curves in front instead of having the straight edge it was born with. It's almost unnoticeable to me. Almost. But I can't help myself. Each time I look at that lost corner, I think of rabbits, which I have a newfound awareness of. Tim asked me to babysit his rabbits ("They're soooooo cute!") the last time he went to visit his mom in Cleveland. I declined, remembering "the courage to change the things I can and the wisdom to know the difference!" It was a bigger responsibility than I wanted.

How's this for a segue? Have a healthy awareness of your clothes. They may be soooooo cute, but remember, you're responsible for them once you get them home, so be prepared to care for them the best you know how.

Don't Pack Trouble

*Overpacking
gets way out of control when
individual pieces won't cross over
to help another outfit out.*

YOU KNOW THAT PUBLIC SERVICE ANNOUNCEMENT on TV where the guy—mean, like he was your high school principal—says, "This is your brain" and he shows a cast-iron skillet. Then he cracks an egg into the hot skillet and says over the loud, fierce sizzling, "This is your brain on drugs." Fried. "Any questions?"

I'd like the same kind of public service announcement about packing a suitcase for a trip.

Here's some edited footage of that announcement. It would start out showing a suitcase packed sensibly. Then it would switch (sizzle, sizzle) to the suitcase packed in haste. (You're in deep doo-doo.) It would show the poor schmuckette starting to pack at 11 P.M. the night before the next morning's 6:30 A.M. departure. Tired, stressed, and with no time to think this through, the poor dear throws in an extra jacket, two extra pairs of shoes to

158

go with the two extra outfits she threw in at the last minute, plus two more sweaters, all *just in case*. Oh, and before closing and zipping the suitcase, she throws in the sunscreen *just in case* she gets a minute to hang out at the pool during convention week in Southern California.

Flip ahead to footage shot after the victim departs the plane at her destination city. She wrecks her elbow heaving the deadweight of this suitcase in and out of airport shuttles. Once at the hotel she goes to unpack and finds the sunscreen has opened during flight. The lotion is all over her clothes that are jammed in tightly. Everything she pulls out is wrinkled and smeared with smelly sunscreen. Before the week is over she figures she ended up using twenty five percent of what she brought and she feels like a failure.

This, or nearly this, has happened to anyone reading this book at this moment.

The *EPA*

Now I believe that anyone who can pack a suitcase with thought and care, and have a wardrobe that works when they arrive at their destination deserves the highest award given out to people who travel: the Excellent Packer Award (EPA).

Someone might say, hey come on, packing a suitcase isn't calculus. No, it's harder. It's a brain twister that can take weeks to figure out, and you're always wondering if you will get it right. No, EPA winners deserve a medal, a star named for them, a mention in Liz Smith's syndicated newspaper gossip column — "Jane Seymour was having lunch with (you the winner) and they discussed (your) EPA," the article will say. Everyone wants to meet you, be your best friend, be *you*! Frenzied fans want to watch you pack. Everyone wants to interview you on TV — Barbara Walters, Elsa Klench, Charlie Rose, Matt Lauer (lucky you!).

If you agreed to an interview, here's what the adoring public would see if they could watch you pack your suitcase for your next trip:

Because you know about this trip in advance, you think ahead. Where will you be in your cycle while you're gone? How many tampons do you need to bring? Speaking of cycles, you'd remind your fans that you also need to plan ahead for those things you really don't want to be trying to find in other cities: hair stylists, colorists, manicurists. It's awful if the day you're leaving, you realize your hair just turned into a bush and it's been over six weeks since you got it cut. While you're at it, I advise getting a fresh manicure and pedicure and bringing your nail colors with you for touch-ups.

You already have duplicate sets of grooming and makeup products, so you don't have to repack these every time. They are in leak-proof bags that close securely, because the airplane pressure makes things leak. (Remember that sunscreen!)

A week or so before your trip, you start thinking about what clothes are going to work for where you're going and what you'll be doing. You carve out one end of your closet as a workspace, or you set up a temporary rack and start pulling the clothes you're considering for your trip. Time is your friend in packing, not your enemy. You look at your collection, edit some things, add others throughout the week.

You're the expert and you know that working with neutral colors is **really efficient.** That's what you'd tell Charlie Rose. "Charlie, I pick a dark and a light neutral. Darks (black, navy, coffee brown, or olive) teamed with lights (taupe, white, ivory, or light gray) are colors you can be around for long periods of time and not get tired of them. Dark colors are easier to dress up or dress down while on the road. Bright colors are quick burnouts. Lime green or hot tangerine would have anybody scraping the hotel walls with their fingernails by day three of an eight-day trip."

You tell how you plan for variety and spunk with color and pattern in your accessories—print scarves, leopard print belts, colorful caps, or headbands. You throw in that lime-green T-shirt or the colorful retro paisley shirt for refreshing accents if you have room in your luggage or are accessory shy by nature.

While looking at those clothes hanging on your working rack, you consider fabrics. Great travel fabrics are ones that bounce back after being crushed. They include crepes or knits, tropical weight wool or matte jersey, denim, microfibers, synthetics, and synthetic blends. This is not the time to insist on your favorite delicate, high maintenance clothes. Leave them at home to entertain themselves while you're gone.

The EPA Planner

Now it's time to get a plan on paper. (Matt Lauer is going to love this part.) Get out pencil and paper and make a grid. On the left-hand side, from top to bottom, list parts of an outfit: outerwear, top, bottom, shoes, underwear, accessories. Now across the page, create a column for all the days you'll be gone. Five columns for five days, or ten columns for five days if day and night activities are different and require a change of clothes. (Matt's going to start whining. He'll say, "Gosh, do you really have to do the math here? Where's the spontaneity? You're going on vacation!" And

you'll say, "Matt, there's plenty of time for spontaneity once you reach your destination. Plan now, play later. Come on now, stay with me.")

Play with these charts. Go through the outfits. Do a practice run. Try on the complete outfits and if you're satisfied with them, start filling in your chart. Write it out from head to toe including all accessories: belts, jewelry, shoes. You assure Matt that you may not follow this written plan exactly (allowing for spontaneity and all that), but just doing it will keep you calm and confident. *And* because you planned it out, when it comes to packing your suitcase the night before you leave and it seems like there's so little there and you wonder if this really is enough to bring, you look back at your plan and remind yourself that you're set! You've worked it out! If you end up mixing and matching in ways you hadn't considered, great.

Winners of the EPA award have tricks to help others think creatively and efficiently. You don't disappoint us. You say, "Think threes." You tell us to see if we have three ways to wear each item we are bringing. Overpacking gets way out of control when individual pieces won't cross over to help another outfit out. Or, you say, think about planning your wardrobe from the bottom up. See if you can get by with three pairs of shoes and create outfits just based on which shoes you want to travel with. You remind the interviewer that if we've shopped for new clothes, we need to be sure we've worn them a couple of times so we know how they'll perform. It's best to work with clothes that we're used to. It's harder to predict how new shoes or new clothes will hold up. And don't forget to plan on something really comfortable to wear on the plane. On departure day, wear your heaviest shoes on the plane and your thickest jacket. Carry a shawl as a blanket and stuff a pair of socks in your carry-on because the plane can be very chilly. Carry your jewelry with you also. Your clothes can get lost and replaced much easier than your favorite jewelry can.

When Liz Smith calls for an exclusive print interview, you let her in on a couple of little secrets: An easy-fitting print dress in a fabric that comes crinkled already is a great traveling companion. Dresses are cool in heat, the print will keep it from showing dirt, and packing is never a problem because it has its own permanent wrinkles. Dress it up with a strand of pearls (fake ones if you're nervous about traveling with good jewelry). Keep it sparse for a dressed-down look.

And then you share with her a hand-me-down tip from one of my clients whose theory is: who cares much what she's got on when she's traveling overseas? It's not like she's going to run into anyone she sees, so she takes clothes from her wardrobe that are headed out of her closet because they are a little dated and are being replaced with more current styles, but they are still in great shape. She gets another year or two out of these clothes by putting them aside in another closet and pulling from them for her travels. If something happens to them, she doesn't care. By updating the outfits with current shoes and handbags, she wouldn't freak out if she *did* run into someone she knew from San Francisco while vacationing in Barcelona.

No matter what anybody says about the weather where you're headed, always pack something for extremes. We all know this one. Your mother assures you that it's hot back home, five states away. "Oh, Honey, it's going to be hot." Because you planned for extremes, you've got the jacket packed and ready to go for the unseasonable cold front that moved in just before your plane landed. Pack something for extreme heat, and pack a cardigan or jacket (a microfiber one will be water resistant and act as a raincoat as well as a windbreaker) for a sudden cold burst.

Now you have your plan, you've done your run-through. Your wardrobe is tweaked to perfection. And you've got time to spare because packing is three days away.

Bring the Camera Crew In for Close Ups

Now packing. It can be done a couple of ways. One way is to hang complete outfits on dry cleaner hangers (jacket, blouse, pant, or skirt) and cover them in dry cleaner plastic bags as long as the garments. Lay them flat and fold them up in a suitcase that has the hooks for hangers or just fold the outfits in thirds and lay them in the suitcase with hanger and all. When you get to the hotel, unzip the suitcase, unlatch the hangers, hang them in the closet and voila, you're ready to go with not one wrinkle. You've taken a lie detector test about those wrinkles. I know you passed.

And now, you dazzle your viewers with this one, the I-can't-believe-it-didn't-wrinkle trick that works in any rectangular suitcase. Open your suitcase, look at it, and identify where twelve o'clock, three o'clock, six o'clock and nine o'clock would be. Take your first top and lay it across the bottom of the suitcase at twelve o'clock, and let whatever doesn't fit naturally inside the suitcase, hang outside of the suitcase. This would be of course, the long sleeves of the top. Then at three o'clock, lay a pant inside the suit-case and let the legs hang out over there past the nine o'clock area. Then go to the six o'clock spot and put down your next clothing item. Go around your suitcase/clock like this until every-thing is lying on top of each other. Then, starting at any o'clock and working clockwise, fold in those parts of your clothes that are hanging over the edges of your suitcase, one end at a time. Twelve o'clock folds into the suitcase, then three o'clock, six o'clock and then nine o'clock. When you get to your destination, fold those pieces out and then pull them out and hang them up. They will be wrinkle-free, or at least nearly so. This most cer-tainly works! You'll bet anybody your EPA award that it does and you'll win every time.

Here's what truly makes you a winner above all others. You have the cure for sterile hotel rooms (or stuffy extra bedrooms at Aunt Hilda's farmhouse in Wyoming) and it's called the Little Personal Care Kit. This is sort of like packing your blanket. You want to pack a few items that will help you create a personal space, take the edge off of generic temporary spaces. Pack small-ish art reprints on thin poster board in your front flat zip pocket. Stash a colorful scarf that you can wear, yes, but also that you can drape over a table, a lamp, or to cover the TV if that seems to be the only room decoration. **Pack a package of tea-light candles and a couple of little candleholders for ambiance.** Make them scented candles to get rid of that hotel smell. Bring a small hand-ful of pushpins to hang up greeting cards or family pictures that are meaningful to you.

With all this thinking ahead, it's no wonder you can forget your troubles, forget about your clothes, and have nothing but a great time.

Don't Pack *Headaches*

Being as thoughtful as you are, you have a simple list of ideas to help someone start thinking about his or her next trip.

Here are key ingredients for a sample travel wardrobe:

A dark suit with matching pants and skirt in a tropical wool. (Resist the temptation to wear sweats or jeans if you're traveling to Europe. Don't give anyone reason to pick you out as an arrogant American.)

A twin sweater set. A sweater set is great for layering. The short-sleeved or sleeveless first layer can be used under the jacket. The twin set can be worn alone with the skirt or pant on alternate days.

T-shirts. Wear cotton for day, silk for dressing up.

Evening pant. Try a drapey chiffon palazzo pant or a shimmery cigarette pant.

Accessories. Take a small silk square scarf in an animal or colorful print to tie around your neck, pretty necklace and earrings for dressing up, casual earrings, a tote or backpack for day, a small fabric or evening bag for night, dressy sandals for night, walking shoes, daytime sandals, sunglasses.

You remind us to do one more thing: Pack our wardrobe plan in our carry-on bag. If our luggage gets lost or stolen, we can use this as documentation for reimbursement by the airlines or our insurance company.

The only advice I have for you after winning your EPA award is to get yourself an unlisted phone number. The media won't let go of you until next year when (and if!) another recipient is announced and you're finally getting a rest! Did I say congratulations? Congratulations!

The Wimp's Guide to Tattoos

Tattoo art doesn't move from room to room. It stays right where it was applied. Forever. People who get tattoos know how to commit.

THERE'S THIS THING I'VE NOTICED, and it's that when the weather changes, people get ideas in their heads to try new things. October winds blow in a cold front and you wake up from a sound sleep announcing, "Today is a good day for a tattoo." And it just might be, but there's a lot more to this than permanent ink. The same way I've asked you to be thoughtful and true to yourself with your wardrobe is especially important now that you're thinking about tattoos.

It's really easy to get a bad tattoo. Let me tell you how.

1. Get drunk.
2. Go to a flash shop and look at the wall of pictures. Take thirty seconds before pointing to the picture of the tattoo you will have forever.

3. Know nothing about the artist doing the work and don't look at his portfolio.
4. Wake up in the morning, look at your tattoo, and say, "Wow, what a bad tattoo."

Now that's probably a pretty good stereotype of getting a tattoo, but let me blow it up. First of all, if you're thinking about getting a tattoo, you've been thinking about it for a long time. It's an urge that won't go away. You've done research on the image you want and maybe even the artist you want to do the work for you. You know what to expect, how to take care of it when you get home and in the weeks to follow. And if you don't know these things, you're about to.

Major cities have the major tattoo artists. In San Francisco, maybe the tattoo capital of the United States, artists are turning to tattoos as a medium to perform their art and the number of good artists is growing. Some people collect beautiful art by artists they admire. Some people collect beautiful art from artists they admire and that art is applied to their bodies. Those of us who collect art for our walls can take it down if we tire of it, or we can move it to another part of our house if we want.

Tattoo art doesn't move from room to room. It stays right where it was applied. Forever. People who get tattoos know how to commit.

The desire for a tattoo often starts with an image. You'll think, "This is a beautiful image to me and beautiful enough that I want to own it and wear it." Images aren't always symbolic. They can just be pretty to you, or amusing. That image on you makes you very unique.

In a world where worrying about what other people think is something nearly everyone deals with, wearing tattoos brings the issue from the inside to the outside. Barbara says, "This is who I am. This is how I choose to look. It takes more self-confidence and comfort to walk down the street and not worry about what people are thinking. It's really helped me get past my insecurities. I have found a place where I know that I'm unique. I love clothes. I dress well. I can go through five outfits in the morning like everyone else, but ultimately, what I put on and how it looks with my tattoos, that makes me *me*."

Sarah enjoys the feeling of ownership she has through her tattoos. She adds, "I own my body. It's mine. I take care of it as I see fit, adorn it as I see fit. It aids in my self-concept. I created the tattoo and no one can take it away from me. It's a living art project."

Some women start out with a tattoo that is not visible to others (the back is a popular spot for women who want to be heavily tattooed but want to put them away and hide them.) That feeling, however, may evolve, and eventually you may find yourself wanting tattoos that are visible.

Picture This Forever

If you've been thinking about tattoos, you have already done a lot of work before you walk into a tattoo parlor. Either you have decided on the image you want and you've been to the library and researched this image and gotten pictures of it from every angle to present to your artist who renders several drawings of it, or you've settled on an artist that you've admired and you know that your taste is a match. Tattoo artists are true artists and they will have specialties. Some artists do great pop-type art; others are great at small, really detailed designs.

Either way, you've researched your artist. You've asked to

see the artist's portfolio. Look for the colors in the photos. You want to see resilient colors. Create a dialogue with the people in the shop. Get a feel for their professionalism. In buying clothes, you want to love what you're buying. Same with tattoos. "That'll work" or "it'll do" doesn't work and won't do. Not for you. You want to be hit with the smell of hospital when you enter a tattoo parlor. Don't trust a place that doesn't smell like disinfectant. The artist needs to be pulling needles out of a package and throwing them away when done with them.

You've considered the artwork itself, its style, where you are going to place it, how it will look on that part of your body. If you are fitting a new tattoo in with some that already exist, on your arm for instance, expect that the artist will place tracing paper over the area of the body that is going to be tattooed to see how it will fit in that space.

Once you get one tattoo, it will probably want company. Yes, it's painful, but when you walk away and start admiring it every day it just makes you want to go get more. That's the way it is. When you start out with one rose at your ankle, the sky seems like the limit. But once you've done three-quarter sleeves on your arms (a sleeve is the area from your shoulder to your wrist, a half sleeve is from your shoulder to your elbow), your lower back is done, and your upper back has a big tattoo, finding another place starts to be a lot like the San Francisco housing market—tight.

You're the canvas; your artist is the Picasso. As more and more artists are surfacing who are really good, you may want to reserve space on your body for their work. If you want something of theirs, start planning for it, realizing that what you choose is very important because it takes up space that could be used by another artist. Once you've run out of room, you've run out of room. Make your choices carefully.

Some people may plan a full out sleeve from start to finish. Other people will add as they go along in which case each new tattoo needs to connect and flow with those that came before. You view things differently as you get older, so your taste may have changed since you got your first tattoo. A good artist can help you bridge your youth with your adulthood.

Tattoo Balancing

When you're adding tattoos, you need to think about scale. If you are balancing a bigger, brighter, more colorful tattoo from an opposite arm and what you're working with is a tattoo of little love birds, someone has to look at that and know how to built a scene around those love birds that will be similar scale to the pop art on the other arm. While you're working this out, take marking pens and do some drawing to help you visualize it or have someone do it for you. Look in the mirror. See if you can imagine it.

The more tattoos you get, the more balance becomes very important. If you put a tattoo here and then another one there and scatter them, the whole of it might not be great at all. Art principles, folks. You need them now. Barbara knew she wanted a tattoo on the back of her lower leg. But she also knew she wanted it to look balanced, so she planned in pairs. One on the right leg, one on the left leg. Different tattoos, but similar in size and scale.

There are plenty of sources for images—tattoo magazines, internet sites, art books, even print ads in magazines could give you ideas. Those have already been through some art directors and may be what you're looking for. Looking through tattoo magazines can also help you visualize bodies so you can make a decision about how far you want to go with this. Do you like the look of a half sleeve? A full sleeve? One arm, both arms?

It's My Tattoo and I'll Cry If I Want To

Pain. Okay, I've avoided talking about this as long as I could, but it's time. Any area that you think will hurt most likely will. Where skin is tender, like the inside of the arms, inner thighs, behind the knees, elbow, lower back, it's *painful*. Next to bone hurts bad. This would include the area next to your shoulder, your back, kneecaps, over ribs, shins. Where there's more meat, it's usually less painful. The more you get tattooed, the more you are familiar with the pain and maybe you can tolerate it more.

Wondering how to manage the pain? Engaging in conversation with your tattoo artist is one way. Breathing is another. Pull out your Lamaze breathing if you've been through childbirth. Rather than tensing up and holding the pain in, be aware of it and let it flow out of your body. Imagine a calm, peaceful, beautiful place. Try to go there for thirty seconds at a time. Be there instead of in the pain. A two-hour stretch is a good sitting and represents a lot of ink and a lot of work. If you are flying to a major city to work with an artist, you will be more psyched into getting the whole job done at one time if you can, so you'll want to pace yourself.

There are three processes that have to be done. Outlining, shading, and adding the color. Most people say that the outlining or "line work" isn't so bad. If you have sketched the face of your grandmother and want it on your arm forever, the ouch level is low. If you want to add in how she used a lot of rouge on her cheeks, had a blend of blond and gray hair and you want to get that just right, and you also plan to showcase her purple-blue eyes, you're in for more pain. The filling in of color is where the pain is. If you're doing "washes" where you go for a translucent look, you'll be going over a spot two or three times and that gets a bit testy for the pain threshold.

Most people who get tattoos have been thinking about this for years, fine-tuning the design. It's all that dreaming time that makes the pain manageable. When it's over, you look over and there's your beautiful, personal work of art, on you. You should be beaming and saying, "Ouch, thank you!"

It's best to put two weeks between appointments. And, gosh darn it, stay out of the sun after you've been to the parlor. Getting a new tattoo sunburned is extremely painful.

For the first week you have to keep it moist. If you can keep it bare and moist, that's even better. Otherwise your clothing will suck up all the soothing ointment. Putting clothes over that area is going to be pretty tough for a week or so. It'll be very sensitive, then it'll dry, peel, crack, and in two to three weeks, the scab will fall off. You need to keep lotion on it.

Moist Is Better

Let's talk maintenance. Sun is very damaging. Without sunscreen, the outline fades. That's how those black lines can fade to blue. And you can lose color too. Sunblock is even more important to you now than ever. And even when you're not in the sun, it's important to keep your skin hydrated.

There are some things you won't be able to do once you've had a tattoo besides take your shirt off in front of Mom if she's freaked out about this. Because you've been exposed to a situation that involves blood diseases and needles, you won't be able to give blood.

If you want to show off your tattoos rather than detract from them, you need to think about your clothes. Now you have this visual thing on you that you wake up with every morning. Adding patterned clothes to pattern on your skin may be too much. Wearing simple clothes or solid-colored clothes will show off the tattoos, letting them be center stage. Tank tops and sleeveless tops show off tattooed arms. And when you're not in the mood, you can cover them up with long sleeves.

Ever wonder what to do when you see a woman with beautiful tattoos? It's okay to comment, but remember your manners. Chris says, "If I have my tattoos out, I expect people will look and be interested."

While you're at it, do some research. If you see a tattoo on someone that you particularly admire while standing in the grocery line, ask her who did it. People are proud of their ink. Fellow tattoo clients are pretty chatty about their experiences.

You have to expect stares, but you also will attract interest and people who admire the work of tattoo artists—not a bad group of people to attract to yourself!

Confessions of a Fashion-Maven Snob

The minute that gazillion dollar designer outfit slithers down the fashion runway in Milan or Paris, someone back home in the United States is knocking it off in their own factories for a lot less.

HOW CAN I SAY THIS without sounding like an utter snob? Lord knows, it's not my mother's fault. She didn't raise me to be this way. I just acquired these traits over the years, all on my own.

I have a thing about retail pricing. It doesn't bother me. I can pay full-price for something and not flinch. In my defense, I know that whatever I purchase I will wear the heck out of, so at nearly any price it becomes a bargain for all I put it through, cost per wear.

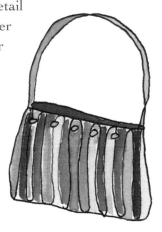

I can never compete when pals start boasting about great shopping adventures where they picked up a terrific coat for fifteen bucks. I go blank. It's like me being in the company of a bunch of Deadheads rehashing Grateful Dead concerts, "Remember the Mother's Day show in Ithaca, 1977? Man, they killed! They were smokin'!" I missed it all—the drugs, the tie-dye, the swaying . . . *and* the bargains. I have no memories of great scores at the bargain basement; standing in line at 7 A.M. for the opening day of a half-yearly sale, or getting a real steal at the Nordstrom Rack.

I'm a retail shopping snob who prefers the higher-end department stores. I shop during the week, when not many people are there. I don't like crowds. There's no line for a dressing room. Merchandise isn't crammed onto floor space like the gymnasium floor seconds after the winning basket of a high school basketball championship game between rival schools. Put me in a high-end department store or a classy boutique with shocking sticker prices and I'm at home—comfortable, calm, composed. If they have to price those clothes high enough to pay for the privilege of walking around arty displays with room to spare, then let me just get out my checkbook and help them continue that policy.

So, then, how did I get caught by Robin, a sales associate I know well from one of those high-end retail stores, while standing in a crowded discount store with a mound of clothes heaped in my arms, only a few steps from the checkout counter with lies coming out of my mouth?

Easy. A friend got me into this mess. Not just any old friend, but a friend who owns two women's retail stores. How she explained it to me was: she was shopping with her finicky college-aged daughter at a discount store. While she was biting her tongue to keep from offering her daughter her immense knowledge on the subject of what would look great on her, she poked around the racks looking at things she might be interested in for herself. That's when she spotted the perfect pair of pants. She bought three pairs. "See these," she said, pulling on one of the pant legs of a pair she was wearing one day, "this is one of them. Eighteen bucks. You should check them out!"

Three days later, I'm getting a prescription filled in a drugstore at the discount end of town and I decide to sneak a peek. It takes some focus with everything jammed tight on the racks. (More space between hangers means these pieces are really "special." The more expensive the clothes, the fewer of them are hanging on a rack.) But I know how to focus in a store. I'm a professional!

I spot a skirt style **I've been wanting to try** and some shirts in my colors. Then I see knit long skirts and matching tops, outfits that are **exactly** what I've been wanting to wear this fall.

I can't choose between the black and olive, so I pull them both. After all, they're cheap! Pretty soon, I'm in a dressing room doing for me what I do for you, creating a high functioning wardrobe; focusing on fit and getting separates to work with each other.

After careful consideration, thinking it through like I ask you to, I head ecstatically for the messy, cluttered checkout counter. That's when I see Robin, the sales associate from the *other* store, and just like when your foot slips out from under you and you know you're going down, I could see that she couldn't help but run right into me. She was walking fast. She probably didn't notice how the color palette of items under my chin all looked like they could have been perfect for . . . me!

Her eyes grew wide and she said, "Brenda, what are YOU doing *here*?" With my friend in mind, I said what any high-paid personal shopper caught in the headlights of the fashion police would say. "Oh, you know me. Shopping for a client. You know, I shop everywhere for these folks. Just another day in the life of . . ."

She looked at me quizzically and sped off before I could finish my fib. I tried to hurry things along at the checkout stand. But when the lady told me I could get ten percent off of my total purchase price plus the thirty percent off of several items if I opened a credit card account, I got sweaty under my armpits, said yes, and stood there watching the door while they re-rang the whole thing. Grand total: $186.

I've never experienced such sticker shock in my life. $186 for twelve pieces of clothing? It was incomprehensible! Yet they acted like this was a big purchase. That $186 might have bought an underwear set at a high-end department store.

I went home and pulled my purchases out of the plastic bags without handles. They give you really wimpy bags at these lower-end places, not the graphically gorgeous couture extra-sturdy bags you get at the big bucks stores.

I pulled out the $18 cashmere tank top that looked just like the one a client of mine bought for $150. She loved it, wore it endlessly, got well over $150 worth of value from it. I felt sick to my stomach with guilt for finding this one six times cheaper. I felt like I'd done something wrong!

I wore that cashmere tank top a week later—with the skirt I bought for $26, and one of the new shirts worn open, creating that dressed down casual chic look while I went off to do a pre-shop for a client. I ran right into Robin again, this time at her workplace. I was mortified that she might recognize the clothes I was wearing as the ones that were in my arms a few days earlier. I hid behind one of those perky displays until she followed someone into the dressing room.

Am I converted to discount stores? No. I will probably continue to be a slave to *full retail.* But what I was reminded of is how fashion works. The minute that gazillion dollar Prada outfit slithers down the fashion runway in Milan or Paris, someone back home in the United States is knocking it off in their own factories for a lot less. You see this especially in the spring when all eyes are glued to the TV sets the night they air the Oscars. Actresses are wearing dresses that are in the same price range as houses in Minnesota. Those gowns are studied by lower-end manufacturers, patterns are made and fabrics chosen, a detail or two may be different, but you could easily wear that Gwenyth Paltrow pink gown at your evening spring formal event two weeks after the Oscars for a couple of hundred bucks.

There aren't copyrights in fashion, so all is fair in the retail world. Knockoffs appear in the stores nearly neck-in-neck with the originals. They're just not in the *same* stores. You're not a fool for buying your favorite designer clothes at full price as long as you love them and wear them. And don't let me mislead you either. It's not all a picnic in the discount stores. No, you have to hunt for what looks like quality. Some things look and feel cheap. The fabric isn't usually the same, the workmanship is not as precise, the linings not as well constructed, the buttons not as classy (although you can upgrade those yourself at a great fabric store). But, to be honest, that $26 skirt looked every bit as great as the $250 version I'd seen the week before.

While you can find any current trend in every price point, here's the key. Check out the high-end stores. Study their goods. Try things on if you have time. Think about what pieces you're interested in purchasing. Then when you spot those pieces for less by another vendor and they look comparable, you know exactly what a great deal you're getting.

And then it's all in how you put it together. When I was mixing up the new clothes with those already in my closet, I came up with an outfit I loved and wore like crazy. It was the black skirt from the discount store teamed with a blazer from the high-end store (the fabrics were compatible), with a shimmery orange blouse from a couple of seasons back and a necklace I'd forgotten I had that just looked incredible nestled inside the neckline of the open shirt collar.

I was wearing that outfit one evening while running a meeting under bright lights in a room full of image consultants. I got lots of compliments that night. Was I nervous about getting busted? Yes. Did I confess? No way. The only one I told was my friend who got me into this. . . and of course, you.

Shopping with Kids

or

Where Is the Rest Room? — I Need to Scream *Now*

Because you'll be wowing them with your steady composure, you'll be able to call out a veto vote if lime-green Daisy Dukes (short shorts) make you crazy.

YOU CAN'T SAY I WASN'T WARNED. At the eleventh homework hour, I agreed to help my son type his freshman essay entitled "Advice to Parents." I'm typing away as I read ahead, "Don't pick out your child's clothing. If your kid is the straightforward type, then he will tell you before you even take the shirt out of the bag that he doesn't like it. If he is not so straightforward, he will accept it with an, 'Oh . . . that's nice' and you'll never see it again. This is because kids figure that if Mom picked it out, it has to be the worst article of clothing known to mankind. This, of course, is probably true."

Ouch, I thought. He's so bitter. Must be the age. I didn't let it stop me when the next week I went spring shopping with my daughters. I loaded them into the car and headed for Macy's to shop for their spring clothes. I marched through the girls' department and made some terrific selections: a darling cotton cropped pant with tulips and daisies all over it, and a cute white blouse with a broad ruffle around the neck for Caitlin. Adorable. Plus a couple of sundresses in an old-fashioned gingham print, for both Caitlin and Erin, dresses as sweet as cupcakes.

I hung the clothes in the fitting room for them to try on. I held up the pant for my youngest. "I hate it," Caitlin said.

"Come on, it's cute. You don't hate it. Just try it on."

She tried it on. It was adorable.

"I hate it, Mom. I hate it, I won't wear it."

Where's all this negativity coming from? I thought. I gave her a minute to chill out and turned my attention to Erin. I took the gingham dress off the hanger and handed it to her.

"I'll try it on, but I don't want it. It's stupid," she said.

"Stupid? How can a dress be stupid, Honey?" I purred.

She slipped it on. I was encouraged. I said, "Oh, look. Isn't that darling? I love it!"

"It sucks, Mom," she said.

They left me in the dressing room to hang up their rejects and went cruising the sales floor on their own. They came back with overalls and striped knit T-shirts.

"I don't like these, " I grumbled. "I won't buy them."

Our disagreement turned into a full-blown tantrum—clothes thrown on the floor, shouted words that were heard in the next department, and then the tears. Oh my gosh, the tears. Big tears, stinging tears, followed by darting from the dressing room, running down the stairs, storming out the front door, dashing to the car, getting in, locking the doors, and sobbing, sobbing, sobbing.

I was on the fourth tissue, imagining them tapping on the window, pleading with me, "You're right, Mommy. The dresses *are* darling. We'll wear them on the same day and look alike. Please come back, Mommy, *please?*" They were begging.

When I looked outside, no one was there. What's wrong with them? Don't they know I'm an expert here? It's my *job* to pick out just the right clothes for people. I've been doing it for *years*.

A faint voice from the corner of the sun visor interrupted me.

"So you're a fashion consultant. Treat your kids like you do your clients."

"Are you kidding? I'm spending *my* money here, not somebody else's. I get to say what goes. *It's my money,*" I protested out loud.

*"So you want to buy them clothes they don't like and won't wear. Why don't you just throw money out the window instead? Go ahead, throw it out **right now!**"*

I blew my nose and remembered the cute dresses I bought them last year that they didn't wear—my favorites—and the plaid shorts and crop tops I found stuffed under their beds.

I twisted the rearview mirror toward me and reapplied my lipstick. I got out of the car and headed gingerly for the elevator. I resolved to step through the doors on the second floor and help my nonpaying clients get a wardrobe they'd both like and wear.

I found them preening in front of the dressing room mirror in the bib overalls and knit shirts. I wondered if I had it in me to pull this off.

"Okay, listen up," I began. "We're starting over. What you buy today has to be what you love. Not *like*, but love in a big way."

"You mean like I love Patrick?" Caitlin asked, referring to our pet snake.

"Yes, like Patrick. If you love this overall like Patrick, then find three tops that you can wear with it. You need more tops than bottoms in your closet," I advised.

I looked at their faces. It was like I had said, "Go ahead. Sit on the living room couch while you eat chocolate frosting out of the mixing bowl." They waited for a minute to see if I was tricking them and then they skipped off to the T-shirt racks. I practiced deep breathing.

When they returned with their finds, I pointed out, "The belt on this overall is really cheap. Let's buy you a better one. If we make your shoes and belt the same color as your hair, it'll tie all your outfits together and you won't need as many shoes."

I started to get into it—guiding while listening to what they liked, keeping most of my opinions to myself. We didn't stop until we had the shoes, the socks, and the hair ornaments that went with their new outfits.

In two hours I vetoed only two things—the neon bike shorts and the ripped-on-purpose jeans. I decided I could live with the rest of their choices. They didn't fuss. I'd earned points for not crying.

Once we were home, the girls tore off the tags, put on a Prince CD and performed a fashion show for their big brother, staying up until 10:30 even though it was a school night, laundering everything and rearranging their drawers.

A week went by. Everyday they paraded out of the door in their new clothes, every outfit accessorized with a broad smile. I never found a single piece of clothing under their mattresses, only candy wrappers.

Saving *Money* On *Therapy*

Years later I had my kids do an exercise for me. I gave them each a piece of paper with this heading: "Things I love to do with Mom." I was thinking they might save some money on therapy in their adult years if they remembered doing fun things with their mom in their youth. On the top of each of their lists (without copying each other's papers) was "Shopping for clothes."

I know there's a lesson somewhere in this story that if applied to world conflicts would surely solve them. While I'm trying to figure what that lesson is and get the phone number for the United Nations, feel free to steal these ideas and use them on your own kids. Just keep in mind the basics. They need to love it. Not "kinda like," but love. They know the difference. If they love the color, but don't like the fabric, it stays in the dressing room.

When they take responsibility for their choices, they will learn to **trust themselves** and **gain confidence.**

When they wear what they love, you save money. It's called the new math. If they wear the jean jacket they pick out forty-five times and it cost $45, the cost per wear was one dollar. If they wear that darling gingham check dress once in the dressing room for you and then stuff it in the back of their closet never to be seen again, that $45 dress cost you $45 for its brief wearing. Multiple that by ALL the things you picked out that they won't wear and suddenly it looks downright sensible to not get your own way, doesn't it?

Because you'll be wowing them with your steady composure, you'll be able to call out a veto vote if lime-green Daisy Dukes (short shorts) make you crazy. That's okay. You've got veto power, just don't overuse it. Remember, there are bigger battles out there—turquoise hair, out-of-town concerts, and tongue piercing—which make brown postal pants look charming.

Fashion Calendar for Smarties

*The cold, hard retail truth
is that if you wait until you need it,
chances are it will be gone.*

ALL RIGHT, I WANT TO SEE A SHOW OF HANDS. How many of you have scurried off to the mall in January when you noticed it was freezing outside, hunting for thermal long johns, wool socks, or a cashmere muffler to keep your pretty neck warm and found, alas! bathing suits, lime green and citrus orange thin cotton anklets, and silk neck scarves with pictures of refreshing lemon slices scattered about? Or how about this? Your high school reunion is in mid-July and a week before the event you realize your bathing suit is hideous. You skip off to pick out a new one and instead of finding bikinis, the store is full of wool pleated skirts and matching sweaters.

The cold, hard retail truth is that if you wait until you need it, chances are it will be gone. You have to train yourself to think a season ahead. It's a lot like gardening. If you want daffodils in the spring, you need to be planting them in the winter.

I know you already think the fashion world is against you and that it's mean to expect you to be on a schedule that doesn't match up to the calendar year, but I'm telling you this for your own good.

I don't like it either! I'm a rebel like you are. It's impossible for me to believe when I'm strolling through the neighborhood admiring exotic varieties of blooming gladiolus in early July that life won't be anything other than seventy-eight degrees and sunny. However, after discovering a few years in a row that the fashion world wasn't going to provide me with the great bathing suit selection during the ninety-eight degree/ninety-eight percent humidity heat wave in August, I have changed my ways. I've given up on bathing suits. But not wool socks. I've learned. Those I'll start buying in September.

The simple way to think about this is to start looking at fall fashions when you're the tannest (July and August), December holiday fashions while you're buying your Halloween decorations, spring fashions while you're making your New Year's resolutions, and summer fashions during that Jekyl and Hyde phase of spring when snowstorms can show up on April 15. This you can count on: The fashion year will always be ahead of the calendar year—not to annoy you but to serve you, my dear.

Photocopy this shopping calendar guide (you have my permission), tape it to your closet door, and use it. It tells you what to expect in the stores each month of the year. Take my advice and you'll be one of the smug ones *next* January who's warm and snuggly when everyone else is turning blue.

January
Stores let their stock go low this month because it makes it easier to do inventory at the end of the month. Winter things are on

clearance and spring merchandise is dribbling into every department—crocheted handbags in bright fruity colors, fun colorful summer shoes. Cruise wear is in—flowing print silk pants and linen jackets, straw hats. Spring hosiery colors are in, happy and peppy. Valentine's Day-inspired items appear—red teddies, scarves with hearts on them. If you've been lusting for a cashmere coat, this is the time to pick it up. It'll be thirty to sixty percent off.

February/March

Spring clothes are in the stores in transition fabrics first—those cottons, linens, silks, rayons, and polyesters that are a medium weight in both casual and career clothing. Expect to see colors like camel, khaki, and clear brights like coral, turquoise, and watermelon. Styles start to look real playful. You can't help but fantasize about water-balloon fights and chocolate-dipped ice cream cones. It can be a challenge at this time of year to put a work wardrobe together because everything is saying, "Come play with me!" Best to get out there early for best selections. Mid-March is the pinnacle for spring merchandise selection.

April/May

This is when you find serious summer clothes—sleeveless, skimpy clothes in lightweight fabrics while the late deliveries are again in transitional weight fabrics—clothes that are a little heavier to work into early fall. Navy shows up again because it's a good transitional color. Look for spring clothes on the sale racks. April has the biggest selection of summer clothes.

June

This is the month of summer clearances. If the weather has stabilized and you're just now thinking you'd like to have a couple of frothy summer dresses, run, don't walk to the stores. If you're a famous procrastinator and haven't gotten around to shopping for summer until now, you'll be delighted to run into everything on sale. The cautionary part of this tale is that sizes can be very picked over. Department store salespeople, once very happy to find your item in your size in another store if they didn't have it for you there, will laugh at your request to find it elsewhere. Most likely it doesn't exist elsewhere. Don't throw a tantrum. You're late.

July

Department stores try to wake you up out of your lazy-margarita-poolside reverie by announcing in full-page ads PRE-SEASON SALES. For two weeks they bring out never-before-seen fall merchandise at sale prices to get you in to buy wool. Again, the first wool that comes out is a lighter weight or a silk/wool blend to transition you into the thick of fall. Fall handbags appear in darker colors and heavier textures—leather, suede—and leather gloves are displayed. This can be a great time to score a leather jacket.

August/September

Summer clothes are gone; the floor is loaded with wool and heavy cottons. You'll find long-sleeved turtlenecks in transitional silk blends. Trust me, even though kids are starting back-to-school on the hottest day of the year, it will get cold enough to wear these things. Dive in for prime selection. Fall hosiery colors are in. Don't come later than September for the biggest selection of fall merchandise.

October

The heaviest weight woolens are in—thick sweaters, merino wool tunics and skirts/pants appear, as well as velvet and cashmere. Turtlenecks are in wool. Long johns and flannels are here.

Holiday clothes appear this month and are often picked over or gone by the end of November; what's left is on sale in December. "Holiday" is a particularly short season, so if this is the year you have lots of parties to go to, shop early. Mid-October has the best selection of winter merchandise.

November/December

Resort wear shows up for holiday and winter travel to Hawaii, Mexico, Caribbean islands. Resort influences include nautical colors—navy and white, palm tree prints, chiffon, some sleeveless items. This is not the best time to decide to come up with a core work wardrobe. In fact, "clothes" for day-to-day life aren't as much fun to shop for right now. They are being pushed off the floor space by gift items galore—fuzzy slippers, jammies in lots of prints, and scarves and mitten sets are falling off tables.

Attention, Shoppers— *on Aisle Two . . .*

Because you're going to be the smartest shopper around, here are a few **Smart Shopping Reminders** to go along with your shopping calendar year:

1. Shop early in the season for best selection of sizes and styles.
2. To find spring clothes in springtime, shop the outlet stores toward the end of the spring calendar year. The major stores have shipped their "end-of-season" merchandise to the outlet stores to make room for the next season.
3. If you find hosiery colors in tights, opaques, or trouser socks that match your outfit perfectly, you must-must-must stock up. It's the glue that makes the outfit shine. Nothing else will do. Buy it now.

4. Texture and weight of fabric determines the season, not color. Hot pink can show up in a summer silk or a winter wool melton. Fall colors aren't always fall anymore. Espresso brown is in linen and even though the color is dark, you'll put it away in September or October. Linen is not a winter fabric unless you live in a tropical climate.

5. If you see something, fall in love with it, and say, "I'll go home and think about it," don't spend more than seventy-two hours pondering. Two weeks later may be too late. Some items truly do fly out the door.

Who's the smart shopper now?
You are!
Shop on, sisters.

Myths Exploded into Smithereens

Remember, it never stops feeling good to feel good about how you look.

OKAY, GET READY. You've got some ideas rattling around in that pretty little head of yours that just need to be booted out of there. Time to clean out that lint trap in your brain where you've got some old myths trapped. Time to scoop them out and throw them away. I don't care what your mother or *Vogue* magazine has told you. That was yesterday and yesterday's gone.

Everyone needs to have a little black dress. Bull crappy. Some people just can't wear black. It makes them look ghostly. Remove this rule from your rule book. It's like saying everyone needs to have kids or everyone needs to get married, or everyone needs to wear underwear. Some people aren't cut out for kids, marriage, or underwear. Well, maybe more people are cut out for underwear than for marriage and kids. Anyway, don't let anyone intimidate you like this. There are lots of other choices. Assuming that little black dress is for evening social events, wear other dressy colors. If it's dark and shiny, it'll do the same thing as a black dress. Look at "blackened" darks, colors with black in them that bring the color down into elegant hues. It could be blackened browns, blackened olives, or head toward midnight navy or charcoal. Other dressy colors are light colors—dove gray, ivory, and taupe in shiny or shimmery textures. Metallics are dressy—copper, bronze, gold, silver.

Black can really bring out the wrinkles in a face, pull out dark shadows under the eyes and make the shadows more noticeable. If you are wearing black and it's not enormously friendly to your skin tone, bare as much skin as possible before you get to the black. If it's low cut, your bare chest will bring some relief from bad black. Also, wearing jewelry that is bright will be a nice barrier.

It's—cargo pants, peasant tops, bell bottoms, the grunge look—over. It's not coming back. Everything comes back. Even the bad stuff. Count on it. If you've lived through a trend once, you might meet its second coming with a groan. "Not this again! I never liked it the first time around!" Here's how to deal with that. First of all, you have choice. Reject it if you want to. But dabbling in trends keeps you looking fresh, so consider looking at the reemergence of the 70s disco queen in postage-stamp doses, not head-to-toe. Add colorful wild prints to your sensible clothes in a scarf around your neck or in a playful handbag you fling over your shoulder. Or look at platform shoes and consider buying a modified pair, not four inches tall, but two inches tall, when they come around.

But it—cargo pants, peasant tops, bell bottoms, the grunge look—is coming back. I'll hold onto these things. It all comes back, but always with a different twist or in a new and improved fabric. Relics from another era keep looking like relics. They are cute on teenagers. Old clothes on women over forty makes women over forty look old.

Plus-size women should always wear dark colors to look thinner. Wrong. Wear bright pink, tangerine, yellow, anything you want. Larger women can actually pull off brighter, bolder things if they choose because they have the stature for a bigger statement. Same with big prints. Don't shun them thinking they will make you look big. Put a teeny-tiny print on a large woman and it looks ridiculous—like a grown person in patterned baby clothes. Bigger people, bigger prints, unless the scale of the face is teeny tiny. Then scale down the pattern. If we're looking at a print of full-plate dahlias, bring it down to delicate pansies.

Never wear horizontal stripes. You have to believe me, because I've spoken nothing but truths, but here's a myth buster that you're going to want to argue with me about. I was dressing a woman for her life on her fifty-eight-foot sailboat. We were looking for casual clothes and I found a navy and white striped cotton/Lycra T-shirt. The stripes were going across. I put it on Laurie, who was suspicious of stripes, considering how that rule has been around since cavewoman times and is genetically coded into the psyche of women in all cultures. I said cheerily, "Oh, let's try it on anyway." It was fabulous. Laurie wears a 36 DDD bra. She has an ample bustline and doesn't plan to draw excessive attention to it. So, with this rule in mind, it would have been easy to have rejected it. But the right size and an adventurous nature is everything. The stripes in the shirt were narrow, more elegant than a wide-striped shirt. The size was right and didn't pull across her bustline, but laid relaxed on her. It was perfect. Dive into stripes!

If you're tall, wear flats. Linda is 5'10." As a kid, she always wanted to make herself shorter so she'd "fit in." When her niece came to visit her, they went shopping together. Her niece is 5'8", has done some modeling, and doesn't apologize for being tall. They went shoe shopping. "Linda, you have to have these shoes," she said. They were really comfy, had a strap across the instep, and had four inch heels. Linda tried them on and they were fabulous. She had an epiphany. She's tall. She's never going to be not tall, so time to get over it! Buying these shoes and making herself even taller was a breakthrough. "When I wear them, I get a lot of looks. But I feel okay with it. I'm tall. It's just what's so. I'm embracing it, because it's the truth of who I am. I might as well enjoy it." Whether it's tall that you are, or voluptuous or tiny or angular or curvy, embrace it. Someone across the room is lusting for what you've got.

If you've got hips, you can't wear knits. I hear more women say in shaky voices, "Oh, I have hips, I can't wear knits! They'll show too much." Wrong. You need to find knits that, like anything else, fit you properly. But you can find hearty knits, knits with body, that will outline *your* body without clinging to it. Show those curves! If you're feeling modest about those curves, throw a shawl over the back of you or wear a jacket or cardigan in the same knit. Knits actually can give a better fit than other clothes because they so enjoy following your lead, curving where you curve, lying straight where you lie straight.

You have to know this stuff from birth. You can't **"learn"** style.

Meet Persia. Everyone asks her about her name. She always snaps back, "It's just a name. Get over it." But I know that she was born Debby Jo in Memphis. Before I hired her to work with my clients, I would bump into her at various functions and she always knocked me out with her great style. Her friends look to her for her up-to-the-minute ideas on fashion.

Persia wasn't born with style. She chose it. A defining moment for her was when, in the summer before seventh grade, she attended a workshop sponsored by *Seventeen Magazine*, that came to town. She says, "They gave you feedback on your outfit and then picked one out for you and took a picture. It let me know I would never be a model, but it got me excited about how to make my own fashion look. At the same time, my mom taught me how to sew. She'd give me a buck or two out of the grocery money. I'd go buy a yard of fabric and a zipper and matching thread and I'd whip up an A-line skirt for myself, every week if I could."

Persia, until then, had lived in hand-me-downs. Like many young women, she never got the pep talk at home where Mom or Dad says, "You can do anything, Honey." She says, "I had a tremendous insecurity. I was either completely ignored or caught up in some rage-drama thing that I now see as typical alcoholic behavior. Studying beauty was a way that carried me out of that world. Clothes helped me to feel strong, beautiful, and important. I was seen by my peers when I wasn't seen by my family."

Persia's style revolves around her passion for color. Most of her clothes are in solid colors and classic shapes. She says, "I'm not a fancy shmancy person. No shiny fabrics. I like classic shapes but don't want to look Republican. And then I make it funky." Let me clarify this. It's not "funky" messy, it's "funky" sophisticated/arty/special/unique.

Persia loves colored shoes. She's always scouting for accessories—belts, scarves, sunglasses, bags, shoes, watches—knowing that they will add the punch, the personality to her classic clothing shapes. Against her solid color clothes, she'll add a handbag in a bright, zesty color, like her apple-green leather bag.

What started out as a coping mechanism in an out-of-control family grew into a trademark for Persia that continues to be a source of joy to her and to others. It turned her life around and led her to one of her passions, her professional makeup artistry business. Remember, it never stops feeling good to feel good about how you look. People are entertained, refreshed, and happy to see you. And that only comes back to refresh, energize, and entertain you too. Choose style now—at whatever age you are. Choose it at 17, at 27, 37, 47, 57, 67, 77, and 87. Heck, choose it at 97.

Salespeople are just interested in their commission. Au contraire. A good salesperson makes money on your sales, yes, and what do you get in return? An incredible resource. They are specialists in their product. They get hours of instruction on their merchandise. They know what they have, what's coming in, what fits a certain way. They can be an advocate for you and your clothes. If you run things by your husband because he's your ally and wants the best for you, ask the salesperson of the boutique if you can take it home on approval. They will often say yes. If you don't have a lot of shopping in your area, ask a salesperson where you vacation to send you a care package every season. Building a rapport with a salesperson who "gets" you can be invaluable. She'll know what you have from past seasons, what styles you prefer and will look out for your wardrobe. Cultivate that relationship. They can jump through hoops for you.

Be fair. If you are "just looking" be up front about it. Don't keep it a secret. Don't keep them engaged when they could be working with a buying customer.

I can't find any pants to fit me. Everyone thinks they are so special and their problems are unsolvable. Sometimes the solution is to get in there and just do the grunt work. Even professional shoppers hanging out in dressing rooms kiss a lot of frogs before they find a prince of a pant. Try on twenty-five to fifty pairs. Stop whining until you've put the work in. Don't try three pairs of pants on and then give up.

I don't have a say. Yes, you do. Your dollars vote. Your subscriptions to magazines are a vote. Your e-mails about a magazine or a designer's ad campaigns are a vote. What you purchase and what you leave behind is a vote. Get out the vote!

I'm just a mom. I don't care if you are on the mommy track. It's no excuse for living in stained sweats. Don't tell me I don't understand. I do. I've been there three times. Even if you are in comfy sweats all day, you can still put on something nice in the evenings, like Sally does. She changes clothes before her husband comes home. It marks a break in the routine of the day, and reminds her that's she's a woman too, not just a mom. If you forget yourself for an extended period of time, it's just too easy to carry that neglect on as a habit after the kids are doing a decent job of taking care of themselves. They're doing great, and you look terrible. Taking care of yourself takes care of the whole family.

If I just match the color, I can put these two things together and make an outfit. No—a casual pant in camel isn't going to go with the dressy business camel blouse. It simply doesn't work! Always pay attention to the mood of a garment. Is it casual and friendly? Then you can match colors up if you like. Is it formal and more serious? Then, again, match colors up. If they have opposing views—like Democrats and Republicans—they are best not being put together in the same outfit.

It costs a fortune to stay in style. There are style decisions everywhere. Don't miss an opportunity to express your style. It's that decision you make when you come upon the little $2.98 plastic colorfully designed case that holds business cards. Do you choose the orange one with the alternating rows of circles and squares? The lavender one with the daisy petal design? The turquoise one with cone shapes all over it? Choose the one you LOVE. Create a little mini-office for your purse or tote bag and buy a matching mesh bag with a zipper that will hold your business cards (in that cute case), a small calculator, a pen, a few paper clips, maybe even your mini cell phone. Minus the cost of the cell phone, this little love fest that you look at every time you open your bag will have cost you $15 but will have given you back heaps of fun. Think of all the joy you can have picking out your key chain, your wallet, your umbrella, your computer case, your gloves, your raincoat. Stay awake. Make each choice count. Great choices equal great joy.

Fashion is for the teenagers. I'm giving up. Getting older, gained some weight, think you've lost your fashion sense? Is that your excuse for giving up on looking good? Nope, you're not going to do that. Beauty on the inside is beauty adorned on the outside. Beauty on the outside reminds us of the beauty on the inside. Dressing well isn't so much about clothes as it is about love. Getting dressed consciously is an opportunity to live your love. Seeing others who dress beautifully is a gift. Be that gift to others. Be that gift to yourself.

Buying quality clothes is a great investment because you'll have them forever. I used to preach "investment dressing." The whole idea was that you buy the best quality you can find, preferably a core wardrobe, and those clothes interchanged would last nearly forever.

I don't believe that anymore. I don't even preach it. Oh, I'm for quality. I love it. But what I've learned over the years is that fashion changes and even more than that, we change, so investing the big bucks in a wardrobe to last forever doesn't make sense because you are constantly reinventing yourself.

I'm looking less and less at forever. I don't want clothes to last forever. I'm going to get bored long before forever. What is essential in expressing your character one year could be extinct for you in two years.

If you like classics, are an understated person, and you trust you're going to be close to the person you are now or five years from now, okay, take the risk, go for it. But, I warned you.

If you bore easily, you don't want to do this. If you're a cutting edge kind of gal, you need up to fifty percent of your wardrobe budget to chase the trends. Since these clothes are going to make quick turnovers you may want to consider smart sale shopping to stay current.

They don't make clothes like they used to. There's just nothing good out there. As an image consultant who is in the stores all the time, I can tell you that each new fashion season feels like Christmas. New lines, new designers, new colors, new textures excite and inspire new possibilities in everyone's wardrobe. There is new opportunity for expression. A shimmery fabric can put you in touch with your sensuality and compel you to express more sensuality in your life.

It might be easy to be grumpy when you see new things that you just don't understand. Force yourself to try things on, just for fun. I'm always saying that. "Try this on—just for fun." And then I hear the line used most often in a dressing room with me—

"I never would have tried that on and I love it!"

Sometimes it takes a year before you even notice a trend. If something is introduced in the spring and people buy it, it'll often be translated into something for fall and keep evolving for five years or so. If you don't notice it the first year, no big deal, you'll catch on when it shows up the next year. Be adventurous. The earlier you try it and like it, the longer you'll enjoy it in your wardrobe.

Many years ago, I made the choice to move away from a part of California that I loved so much, because I was nervous about raising my babies next door to a nuclear power plant. I was at a farewell party at a home in the country, nestled in the vineyards east of town where the night sky was lit up by a full moon and more stars than I'd ever seen. I left the house full of people, walked up a hill, and stood alone looking at the sky. I thought about this place and the people I would miss so much and I started to cry.

Soon, I heard a voice in the dark. "Brenda, is that you?" A friend came and stood next to me under those stars. I told her how I was nervous about leaving this beautiful area and the wonderful people I had met here and she said, "Brenda, there are good people everywhere."

She calmed my heart. And, of course, she was right.

I want you to know that in your life with clothes on, there is goodness everywhere. Don't be afraid to leave a style behind because it has become outdated. There are more wonderful styles in front of you that you will enjoy even as much as these that you are leaving.

There are wonderful people out there to help you. There are trusted salespeople that you will get to know and who will guide you with their knowledge of new fabrics, new styles, new colors.

There are image consultants who make their careers out of helping you navigate your new life, who help you maximize your dollars into an efficient wardrobe that brings you confidence, success, and joy. Seek them out.

Nature is constantly offering examples of ever-changing beauty that begs to be noticed and interpreted into clothing choices. Let the fall colors inspire you to wear the golds, pumpkins, rich browns, and deep olives that surround you. Let the springtime daffodils and crocuses inspire you to perk up your wardrobe and celebrate spring. **Be fluid in your wardrobe. Let life move you and direct you.** Don't get hard and stuck and immovable. Be open.

Have courage. It takes courage to get through life. And your best ally can be the depth of understanding that you have about yourself. What strengthens you? What comforts you? When you need to feel powerful, reach for that power suit. It will help your frame of mind to be physically reminded of your intentions. When you need comfort, let those soft fabrics and gentle colors relax those muscles.

It has been my deepest pleasure to be in your closet and your dressing room with you as you get dressed for the many parts of your life. I wish you could see your glorious self through my eyes. I wish for you the pleasure that comes from seeing yourself in the mirror and loving what you see—a true expression of your most current beautiful self.

Remember, your wardrobe is alive as long as you are. **Never give up on yourself.** Be sweet to yourself, kind and generous. **Many blessings** and I hope one day that you'll have your clothes on and I'll have my clothes on and we'll meet each other and recognize our true selves in one another. Until then, **Dear One,** have fun.

About the Author

Brenda Kinsel has been matching people's clothes to their looks, personalities, passions and lifestyle since 1985. She is the owner of Inside Out, A Style and Wardrobe Consulting Company, based in the San Francisco Bay Area.

She has been writing about fashion for nearly a decade, beginning with articles in the *San Francisco Chronicle* and the *Marin Independent Journal*; as the fashion editor for the *Pacific Sun* newspaper; editor of trade newsletters; and most recently, the author of her first book, *40 Over 40: 40 Things Every Woman Over 40 Needs to Know About Getting Dressed.* She has appeared extensively on TV, including The Oprah Winfrey Show and Fox News and she has been featured in the *Chicago Tribune*, the *Boston Herald, The San Jose Mercury News,* and the *Detroit Free Press.* She has appeared on radio in stations all across the country and Canada.

After years of leadership to the field of image consulting through her participation in the Association of Image Consultants International (AICI), Brenda was awarded the most prestigious award in the image industry, the IMMIE (Image Makers Merit of Industry Excellence), in July 2000.

Born and raised in North Dakota, she graduated with a degree in education from the University of North Dakota. Brenda has three wonderful kids (young adults) who are responsible for making her a nut about basketball and jazz, two subjects that don't come as naturally as fashion, but ones she pursues with great enthusiasm nonetheless.

You can correspond with Brenda by writing to: P.O. Box 657, Ross, CA 94957; or e-mail: bkinsel@brendakinsel.com.

About the Designer/Illustrator

Jenny McFee Phillips has been a graphic designer for thirteen years. Her work ranges from developing strategy and launching new products, to creating whimsical illustrations on popular culture.

She is known for her skills in making unfamiliar, difficult subjects intelligible. Her work for organizations has illuminated difficult concepts for a wide audience. Her concepts and designs for cultural institutions in New York and San Francisco have contributed to the increased exposure of a number of arts groups.

Her client list includes Time-Life Books, American Express, The Metropolitan Museum of Art, MTV, Vanity Fair, the American Institute of Architects, GAP Inc., Carnegie Hall, Brooklyn Academy of Music (BAM), NYC Riverside Shakespeare Co., T. Rowe Price, Bechtel, Golden Gate Park and Recreation, and Montgomery Asset Management.

Jenny Phillips is principal of the newly formed JuMP Studio in San Francisco. The studio provides art direction, marketing communications, graphic design, and illustration.

About the Press

Wildcat Canyon Press publishes books that embrace such subjects as friendship, spirituality, women's issues, and home and family, all with a focus on self-help and personal growth. Great care is taken to create books that inspire reflection and improve the quality of our lives. Our books invite sharing and are frequently given as gifts.

For a catalog of our publications, please write:

Wildcat Canyon Press
2716 Ninth Street
Berkeley, California 94710
Phone: (510) 848-3600
Fax: (510) 848-1326
Visit our website at www.wildcatcanyon.com

More Wildcat Canyon Titles

40 OVER 40: 40 THINGS EVERY WOMAN OVER 40 NEEDS TO KNOW ABOUT GETTING DRESSED
An image consultant shows women over forty how to love what they wear and wear what they love.
Brenda Kinsel
$16.95 ISBN 1-885171-42-0

LIFE AFTER BABY: FROM PROFESSIONAL WOMAN TO BEGINNER PARENT
An emotional compass for career women navigating the unfamiliar seas of parenthood.
Wynn McClenahan Burkett
$14.95 ISBN 1-885171-44-7

STEPMOTHERS & STEPDAUGHTERS: RELATIONSHIPS OF CHANCE, FRIENDSHIPS FOR A LIFETIME
True stories and commentary that look at the relationship between stepmother and stepdaughter as strong, loving, and a lifelong union.
Karen L. Annarino
$14.95 ISBN 1-885171-46-3

BOUNTIFUL WOMEN: LARGE WOMEN'S SECRETS FOR LIVING THE LIFE THEY DESIRE
The definitive book for women who believe that "bountiful" is a way of being in this world, not a particular size.
Bonnie Bernell
$14.95 ISBN 1-885171-47-1

AND WHAT DO YOU DO? WHEN WOMEN CHOOSE TO STAY HOME
At last, a book for the 7.72 million women who don't work outside the home—by choice!
Loretta Kaufman and Mary Quigley
$14.95 ISBN 1-885171-40-4

GUESS WHO'S COMING TO DINNER: CELEBRATING CROSS-CULTURAL, INTERFAITH, AND INTERRACIAL RELATIONSHIPS
True-life tales of the deep bonds that diversity makes.
Brenda Lane Richardson
$13.95 ISBN 1-885171-41-2

CALLING CALIFORNIA HOME: A LIVELY LOOK AT WHAT IT MEANS TO BE A CALIFORNIAN
A cornucopia of facts and trivia about Californians and the California Spirit.
Heather Waite
$14.95 ISBN 1-885171-37-4

CALLING THE MIDWEST HOME: A LIVELY LOOK AT THE ORIGINS,
ATTITUDES, QUIRKS, AND CURIOSITIES OF AMERICA'S HEARTLANDERS
A loving look at the people who call the Midwest home—whether they
live there or not.
Carolyn Lieberg
$14.95 ISBN 1-885171-12-9

THE COURAGE TO BE A STEPMOM: FINDING YOUR PLACE WITHOUT
LOSING YOURSELF
Hands-on advice and emotional support for stepmothers.
Sue Patton Thoele
$14.95 ISBN 1-885171-28-5

AUNTIES: OUR OLDER, COOLER, WISER FRIENDS
An affectionate tribute to the unique and wonderful women we call
"Auntie."
Tamara Traeder and Julienne Bennett
$12.95 ISBN 1-885171-22-6

LITTLE SISTERS: THE LAST BUT NOT THE LEAST
A feisty look at the trials and tribulations, joys and advantages of
being a little sister.
Carolyn Lieberg
$13.95 ISBN 1-885171-24-2

girlfriends: INVISIBLE BONDS, ENDURING TIES
Filled with true stories of ordinary women and extraordinary friend-
ships, *girlfriends* has become a gift of love among women everywhere.
Carmen Renee Berry and Tamara Traeder
$12.95 ISBN 1-885171-08-0
Also Available: Hardcover gift edition, $20.00 ISBN 1-885171-20-X

girlfriends FOR LIFE: FRIENDSHIPS WORTH KEEPING FOREVER
This follow-up to the best-selling *girlfriends* is an all-new collection of
stories and anecdotes about the amazing bonds of women's friendships.
Carmen Renee Berry and Tamara Traeder
$13.95 ISBN 1-885171-32-3

A girlfriends GIFT: REFLECTIONS ON THE EXTRAORDINARY BONDS OF
FRIENDSHIP
A lively collection of hundreds of quotations from the *girlfriends* books
series.
Carmen Renee Berry and Tamara Traeder
$15.95 ISBN 1-885171-43-9

INDEPENDENT WOMEN: CREATING OUR LIVES, LIVING OUR VISIONS
How women value independence and relationship and are redefining
their lives to accommodate both.
Debra Sands Miller
$16.95 ISBN 1-885171-25-0

THOSE WHO CAN...TEACH! CELEBRATING TEACHERS WHO MAKE A
DIFFERENCE
A tribute to our nation's teachers.
Lorraine Glennon and Mary Mohler
$12.95 ISBN 1-885171-35-8

THE WORRYWART'S COMPANION: TWENTY-ONE WAYS TO SOOTHE
YOURSELF AND WORRY SMART
The perfect gift for anyone who lies awake at night worrying.
Dr. Beverly Potter
$11.95 ISBN 1-885171-15-3

Books are available at fine retailers nationwide.

Prices subject to change without notice.